STRUIK PUBLISHERS (PTY) LTD
(a member of Struik New Holland Publishing (Pty) Ltd)
80 McKenzie Street
Cape Town 8001

Reg. No.: 54/00965/07

First published 1991
Second edition 1995

10 9 8 7 6 5 4 3

Text © Brian Johnson Barker
Photographs © individual photographers and/or their individual agents as listed below.
Map © Globetrotter Travel Maps

Editor (1991 edition): Peter Borchert
Copy editor (1995 edition): Brenda Brickman
Designer: Odette Marais
Typesetting: Struik DTP, Deirdré Geldenhuys
Map: Reneé Barnes

Reproduction by cmyk prepress
Printed and bound by Tien Wah Press (Pte) Ltd, Singapore

ISBN 1 86825 870 X

PHOTOGRAPHIC CREDITS
Shaen Adey: pages 16, 24, 103 right, 104, 130/131, 150/151 • Daryl Balfour: pages 88, 90,
93 • Anthony Bannister: pages 29, 50 [ABPL], 64 below [ABPL], 95 below [ABPL], 96 above
[ABPL], 112 [ABPL], 115 below [ABPL] • Rey Bresner: page 18 above • Gerald Cubitt:
pages 13, 28, 33, 35, 38 above, 41, 107, 110, 114, 117, 121, 122, 124, 125, 128, 129 below,
142, 148, 167, 168 • Roger de la Harpe: pages 2, 17 [ABPL], 56, 75, 77 [ABPL], 87 [ABPL],
91 above [Natal Parks Board], 91 below, 94, 95 top and centre, 96 below, 99 [ABPL], 100,
105 below • Nigel Dennis: page 76 below [ABPL] • 1820 Foundation: page 22 above •
John Haigh: pages 19, 20 above, 153 below • Lesley Hay: page 42 [ABPL] • Steve Hilton-
Barber: page 23 [South Light] • Johan Hoekstra: page 51 • Walter Knirr: pages 4, 6/7, 12,
26, 30/31, 39, 40, 44, 45, 47, 48, 49, 78/79, 80, 81, 84/85, 108 above, 113, 116, 126/127,
129 above, 140/141, 144, 149, 152, 154, 155 • Anne Laing: page 32 • Rashid Lombard:
pages 11, 18 below, 147 left • Eric Miller: page 37 [South Light] • Jean Morris:
page 109 • Colin Paterson-Jones: pages 20 below, 120, 158, 159 • Marek Patzer: pages 82
[South Light], 83 [South Light], 97 [South Light], 98 • Peter Pickford: Cover [ABPL],
pages 1, 52, 54/55, 57, 58 below, 61, 62, 64 above, 65, 66/67, 68, 70 [ABPL], 71, 76 below,
134, 135 below, 136/137, 138, 139, 143, 156, 157, 160, 161, 166 • Rob Ponte: page 58
above [ABPL] • Herman Potgieter: pages 46 [ABPL], 86 [ABPL], 115 above [ABPL], 118,
132, 162/163 [ABPL] • Alain Proust: pages 22 below, 34, 127 right, 164, 165 • Eric
Reisinger: pages 60 [ABPL], 69 [ABPL] • Peter Ribton: page 146 • Joan Ryder: pages 72
[ABPL], 113 left [ABPL], 135 above [ABPL] • Wayne Saunders: pages 59 [ABPL], 63 [ABPL]
• Leonard Smuts: page 14 • Lorna Stanton: page 10 [ABPL] • Sun International: page 38
below • August Sycholt: pages 29, 36, 74, 92, 102, 106, 108 below • Lisa Trocchi: page 105
above [ABPL] • Mark van Aardt: page 153 above.

[ABPL = The Anthony Bannister Photo Library]

SOUTH AFRICA
THE BEAUTIFUL

SOUTH AFRICA

THE BEAUTIFUL

CONTENTS

THE LIE OF THE LAND

SOUTHERN AFRICA IS a sub-continent of immensely varied land forms and scenery which largely dictate the patterns of settlement, agriculture and industry. Despite this diversity however, the surface of South Africa may be conveniently divided into two major regions, the inland plateau and the coastal plain.

The plateau is the southern termination of the great African plateau that extends south from the Sahara, and consists of basement rocks overlaid by sedimentary deposits that have weathered and decomposed to produce a variety of soils. The coastal plain reaches Africa's southernmost tip at Cape Agulhas and, with the exception of the west coast, which is washed by the cold Benguela current, is generally an area of great fertility.

Between the inland plateau and the coastal plain is the Great Escarpment, a rugged rim of mountains arranged in rows roughly parallel to the coast. These more or less continuous ranges run from the Transvaal Drakensberg in the north, southward to the mighty Drakensberg of KwaZulu-Natal and the Maluti mountains of Lesotho. In some places the Escarpment falls sheer to the plains some 2 000 metres below while the craggy peaks of Mont-aux-Sources, Champagne Castle and Giant's Castle rise to heights well over 3 200 metres.

Further southward the Escarpment continues in a series of ranges through the Eastern Cape, the southern Karoo and, eventually, loops round into Namaqualand. In the Western Cape and extending along the coastal strip known as the Garden Route, are mountains of a different type. Here, where unimaginable geological forces resulted in the breaking up of the single great land mass known as Pangaea, the buckling, stretching and pulling of the earth's crust gave rise to the Cape Fold Mountains.

The mountains of South Africa play an important role in the land's hydrology, water being a principal determinant of vegetation type and, indirectly, agricultural or other development. Because of the prevalent atmospheric circulation, the amount of rain that falls is directly related to the height of the mountains, especially where the massive ranges, such as the Drakensberg, Swartberg and Zoutpansberg are concerned. Unfortunately however, the mountains are not high enough to collect snow, except briefly in winter.

With the exception of the generally well-watered coastal plain, water supply for urban industrial and agricultural development is one of the major limiting factors in South Africa, especially in the interior where rainfall is often scant and irregular. The country has few rivers of any major consequence and many even dry up completely during the long periods between rains. The two largest river systems are the Orange, rising high in Lesotho and flowing strongly westward to the Atlantic Ocean, and the Vaal, which joins the Orange in the Northern Cape. It is on these rivers and a few others that vast storage dams have been built from where the precious liquid is pumped to areas of need.

Page 1: The thatched cottage of Mon Repos, headquarters of the Cape Wine Academy at Stellenbosch.
Page 2-3: A mixed herd of impala rams and blesbok on the grassy slopes of the Umgeni Nature Reserve.
Page 4-5: A member of the Aloe family, the kokerboom (*Aloe dichotoma*) flourishes in the dry part of the Northern Cape known as Namaqualand.
Page 6-7: One of the world's best-known landmarks, Table Mountain is flanked on the left by Devil's Peak and on the right by the lower summit of Lion's Head.

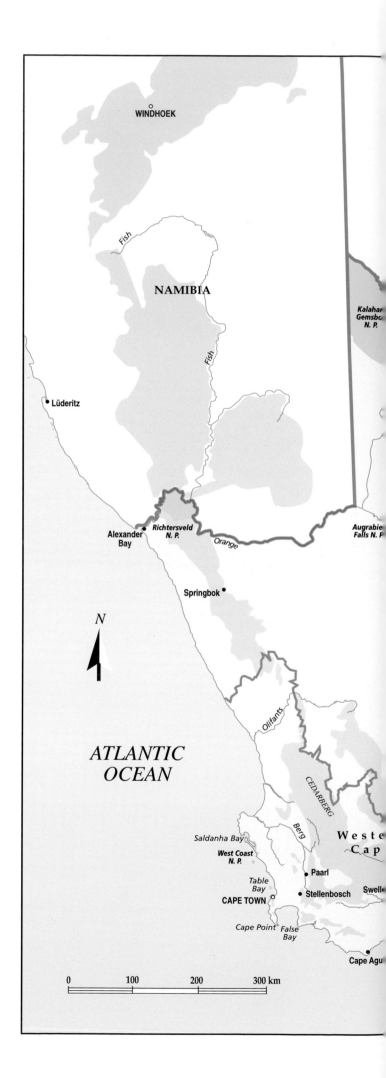

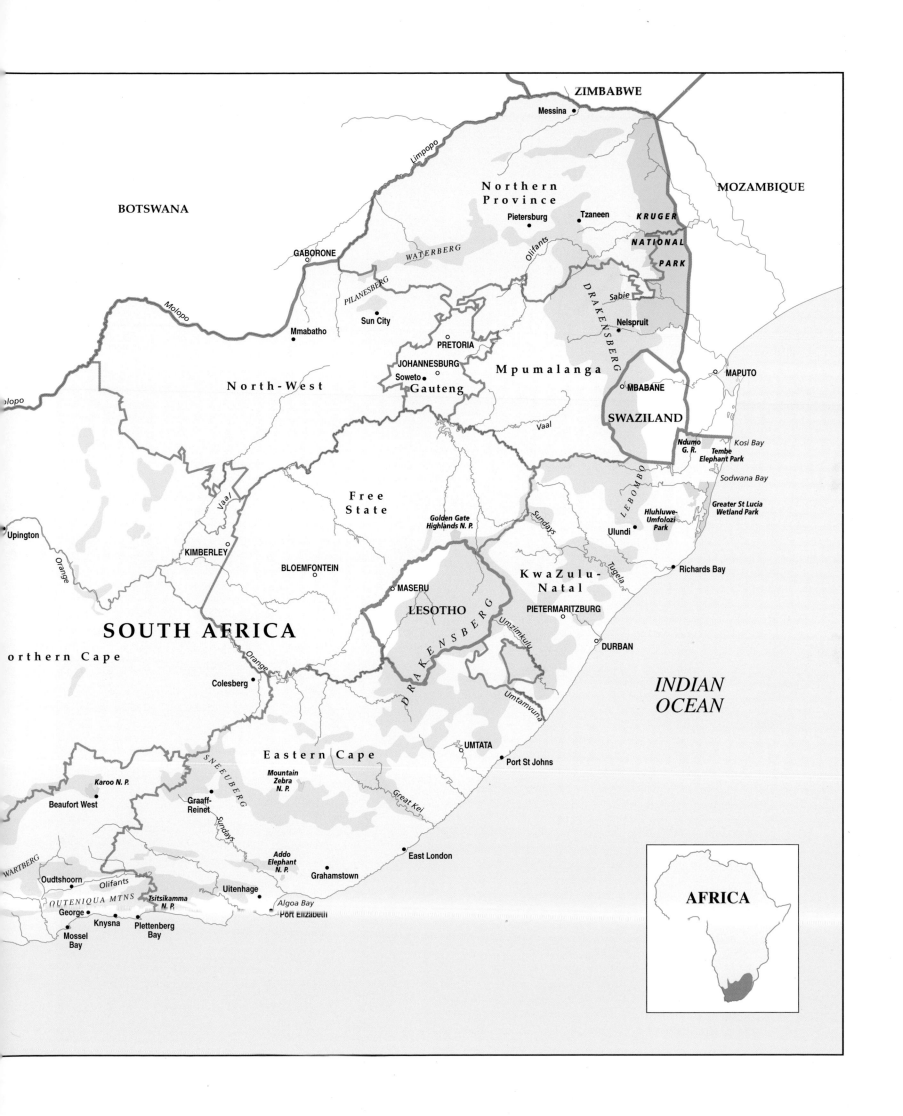

INTRODUCTION

A young girl laughs (above) and the photographer captures a moment of spontaneous *joie de vivre*.

An adult male lion (*Panthera leo*) (left), a grizzled veteran of life in the Kalahari. Lions are renowned for their laziness, but here in the desert they have to work hard to survive. On average, prides in the Kalahari have to make three times as many kills as their counterparts in the Kruger National Park. The reason for this is that game is scarce and lion have to resort to killing many more smaller animals to maintain their high level of protein intake.

MODERN OR WESTERNIZED SOUTH AFRICA may be said to have begun in 1652, when a permanent Dutch settlement was established on the shores of Table Bay. Its development was slow and unequal, until the 19th century discovery of diamonds, and later, of gold brought it to world notice. By then, through the accidents of history and the perversity of individuals, it had already been fragmented into two Boer republics (Transvaal and Orange Free State) of mainly Dutch-descended citizens, and two British colonies (the Cape and Natal) of English settlers and those Boers who were prepared to live under colonial rule.

In South Africa as in other colonized territories – the Americas, Australia, New Zealand – the indigenous people were the losers. They lost land and rights and, to the colonizers, they even lost relevance except perhaps as labour units or, on occasion, enemies to be killed or conquered. But only in South Africa were statute books filled with the legislation of separation and denial. Deservedly, the inequities and inhumanities of apartheid brought South Africa universal opprobrium as successive politicians tried to maintain white privilege, effecting only minor alterations on the sidelines.

The first signs of real change and hope came early in 1990, with the announcement that organizations such as the African National Congress and the South African Communist Party were no longer to be banned. The release of political detainees, of whom the best known was Nelson Mandela, followed and continued over the next year and more. Elections in 1994 brought the formerly banned resistance movements to leadership of a government of national unity, and South Africans look forward to living under real democracy in this truly beautiful land.

At last, great opportunity and the potential to attain the good of all South Africans lies ahead, along a path that few believe will be less than rocky. The unequal divisions of wealth and land need to be addressed justly and fairly, and it is these divisions that, more than anything else, so clearly illustrate the outcome of the loaded policies of the past. But the country has a sound commercial and industrial infrastructure and, with returning foreign investment and a burgeoning tourism industry, the potential to achieve rapid economic advancement for the benefit of all its people.

For a great many visitors, the first close-up view of the country is Johannesburg, a city built on gold and enterprise, greed and exploitation, the inseparable mix common to gold strikes the world over. A little more than a century ago Johannesburg did not exist, its site being a scattering of farms along a patch of veld on a feature known as the Witwatersrand – the ridge of white waters. Men were grubbing for gold in Mpumalanga at Barberton, at Pilgrim's Rest, at MacMac and at Sabie, and a few – just a few – were chipping away on the Witwatersrand, trying to strike the big reef they all hoped really did exist.

It was struck on a day in 1886, by an itinerant digger and odd-job man named George Harrison, on the farm called Langlaagte. Harrison duly received his reward of a free finder's claim – given under old Transvaal law to the discoverer of a new gold-field. It was Claim No 19 and he sold it almost immediately for ten pounds, bundled his few goods into his knapsack, turned his back on the world's most significant gold strike and walked away to the east.

Where he went, and why, or what became of him, is not known. Also not known is exactly which Johann was honoured in the naming of the new mining camp, although several historical figures have their champions. But the city of Johannesburg, in general, is concerned less with the past than with the heady pace of the present, and the acquisition of even greater wealth in the future.

The reef of which Harrison had found an outcrop soon dipped into the complicated geology of hard quartzites and conglomerates, too deep to be worked by the ordinary digger with his pick, shovel and sluice box. What was needed was a vast amount of capital, and an unending source of cheap labour. Capital, at first, came from Kimberley, where the diamond magnates were soon able to encourage further investment from Europe. Labour was supplied by streams of black men from across southern Africa. Only a few adventurous ones, perhaps, came willingly, because the work was hard and dangerous, the underground environment frightening, and the rewards were pitifully small. Most came because they were ordered to do so by their tribal head or had been hoodwinked by labour-recruiting agents. Families were left behind, to manage as they could without the father, or the strongest son, while on the mines the new workers were herded into closed compounds from which – for the duration of their contract – they moved only to go undergound. Conditions in some compounds were undoubtedly worse than in a badly run prison.

Many of the families that the workers left behind failed to make a living as subsistence farmers, and finally abandoned the land to settle in squatter camps around Johannesburg. Women took work for cash wages in the 'white' town that sprang up in the vicinity of the mines. Even in a changing South Africa, the legacy of this migrant labour system remains. Compounds, now far more congenial than formerly, are called hostels, but the disruption of family life remains a sad fact. As South Africa changes, migratory labour will largely disappear, and with it the compounds, but it will take time.

In the very heart of the city, mine dumps and rusting headgear are reminders of the roots of Johannesburg. Horticulturists have tried to soften the starkness of the dumps, and most of these massive heaps now show a summer coat of green as plants reluctantly take root and grow on the unfriendly mineral waste. Another impact of mining on the Witwatersrand landscape has been more attractive – the creation of a chain of dams. This came about through pumping underground water to the surface, and the dams are much used for recreation. Lowering of the sub-surface water table, and the incessant mining have produced instabilities that result in frequent earth tremors, some of them known only by the movement of the seismograph needle. Johannesburg people are philosophical about their tremors, and most regard them with no more alarm than they do the crashing summer thunderstorms.

If the modernity of downtown Johannesburg seems somewhat brash, or even aggressive, wander away from buildings clad in glass or balanced on a central pedestal to find where older structures, some of them almost giants of their day, still survive. The eminent architect Herbert Baker, later to be knighted for his work on imperial New Delhi, opened an office in Johannesburg early this century, and left a fair sprinkling of mansions.for magnates, many of the dwellings – some the size of public institutions – still occupying their splendid sites on Parktown ridge.

Then there's 'the other Johannesburg', adjacent and illustrating the community divisions of apartheid that South Africa is striving to overcome. Soweto – the name comes from SOuth WEstern TOwnships – is home to some two million people. Housing ranges from the informal – that is, shacks and rough shelters – to the near palatial. Until recently, black South Africans in urban areas were regarded as temporary residents whose domicile was one or other of the 'homelands'. They were obliged at all times to carry a pass book, and the harshly enforced 'influx control' laws regulated the numbers who could live adjacent to a white urban area. This has changed, with the scrapping of apartheid laws, and all South Africans may now obtain title to their properties. The Group Areas Act, which demanded that the various races live in their own, separate communities, was repealed in 1991, after having been in force since 1950. But the basic demographic patterns created by apartheid will probably endure for a long while.

T o the north-west of Gauteng, pleasure – and profit – created and sustain the astonishing Sun City and Lost City complex of hotels, casinos, lakes, theatres, and golf courses in a semi-arid area once part of the former Republic of Bophuthatswana. These internal republics – there were others – need some explanation. The ideal of what has become known as 'grand apartheid' was to attain a situation in which there would be no black South Africans. Black people, it was reasoned, belonged to particular groups, distinguished mainly by language, and these groups had traditionally occupied certain areas of the sub-continent. The solution, then, was to return each black person to his particular area as defined by proclamation, and so create a 'homeland' which, in due course, would become an independent republic. Selected citizens would be permitted, under closely monitored conditions, to seek work in South Africa, and, to make the republics financially viable, industrialists were encouraged to establish their factories close to their borders.

Four of these homelands were nominally independent, sovereign states – Transkei, Bophuthatswana, Venda and Ciskei – while several others were known as 'self-governing states'. The cost of this bizarre hegemony, in actual money, in lost progress and, most tragically, in human suffering, was immense. Huge annual injections of funds from the central South African government were required by these states to give their fragile economies at least the semblance of viability. Poverty and unemployment were widespread. South Africa itself, with its former tricameral parliament, also had a triplication of ministries and needless multiplication of administrative costs. Not even unification under a single parliament has been able to eliminate all the artificial complexities of the past. But seldom do these considerations weigh on the mind of the Sun City tripper.

The towering block of the Johannesburg Sun (left), one of the city's numerous modern hotels where excellent restaurants, luxury accommodation and a wide range of leisure activities, including an enclosed jogging course, are the order of the day.

The pedestrian flow is momentarily halted (top) as people wait for the 'little green man' at a busy Pretoria intersection.

The Johannesburg Stock Exchange (above) where shares worth billions are traded each year. Today, 'Diagonal Street' as the JSE is commonly called, is surrounded by the mining-finance hub of downtown Johannesburg, a far cry from the original exchange that was founded in 1887 on open veld.

Whatever one thinks of the architecture, Sun City and the adjoining Lost City are indeed an oasis of sparkling green on the fringe of the Highveld plateau that covers most of the country's hinterland. Initially, most visitors were attracted by the fruit machines and other opportunities to gamble, because these were illegal 'across the border' in South Africa. Some gamblers are still bussed in and out on day trips, and similar opportunities to risk money were created in other homelands. Bids for tourism also saw praiseworthy work done in the field of nature conservation, including the creation of the Pilanesberg National Park around Sun City.

Very different is Pretoria, once the rustic capital of the Boer Zuid-Afrikaansche Republiek and, since 1910, the administrative capital of South Africa. Pretoria is sober and respectable, conscious of dignity and position, and proud of its tidy, jacaranda-lined streets. It developed in more leisurely fashion than Johannesburg, and so had time to provide for green open spaces and more than 100 public parks that include bird sanctuaries and visitor-friendly nature reserves. There are museums too, including ornate Melrose House, where the treaty that ended the Anglo-Boer War was signed in 1902.

This is a university city, with the University of Pretoria the country's largest residential university, while the University of South Africa is thought to be the largest correspondence university in the world.

The buildings of each are substantial, but the most significant structures are probably the Union Buildings, completed in 1910, and the Voortrekker Monument. The Union Buildings, which house the ministries of government, were designed by Sir Herbert Baker for their commanding site on Meintjies Kop. Baker intended them to be impressive, in the manner of a modern acropolis, and magnificently achieved his design, the stately pile being set above an amphitheatre of sculptured gardens and rolling lawns. The Voortrekker Monument was commenced in 1938, centenary year of the event known as the Great Trek but, because of interruptions caused by the Second World War, was completed only in 1949. The Great Trek was a migration by primarily Dutch-descended pastoralists from the Eastern Cape, then the eastern part of the British colony of the Cape of Good Hope. To the Voortrekkers (pioneers), British policy implemented since the occupation of the former Dutch colony in 1806 was vacillating and scandalously liberal, especially in racial matters culminating in the abolition of slavery. This was made worse by increasing competition for land along the frontier between black pastoralists and white pioneer settlers. Their remedy was to yoke their oxen to their wagons, and to seek a place beyond British influence where, in due course, the republics of the Oranje Vrij-Staat and Transvaal (Zuid-Afrikaansche Republiek) were established. In the course of the Voortrekker's search for the Promised Land there were frequent and bloody clashes with the black people of the subcontinent, with victory – and land aquisition – being most frequently a consequence of superior tactics and firepower.

The most successful tactic was a defensive one – the formation of the laager, in which wagons were drawn together and lashed in a circle. This was a flimsy enough barricade, but it provided some shelter for men who without doubt were among the world's finest marksmen. Crude and unreliable though their smoothbore flint-lock muskets may have been, their grapeshot-like effect at short range was more than any enemy armed with spear and ox-hide shield could withstand. Against such a formation, reinforced with cannon, a Zulu army shattered itself on 16 December 1838.

The Voortrekkers, for all their dour faith and their united opposition to things British, frequently quarrelled among themselves. One result of their bickering was that, having reached the Highveld, some followed one leader into the territory that became the province of Natal, while others were led to the far reaches of what was then known as the northern Transvaal. Republics, financially and politically unsound, mushroomed across the map, the most northerly being that of Zoutpansberg, founded in 1848 with its capital at Schoemansdal, below the southern slopes of the 'salt-pan mountains'. Civilization is old here. On the flat-topped, sandstone hill of Mapungubwe – 'place of the jackals' – and on adjacent Bambandyanalo, men were fashioning items of copper and gold perhaps a thousand years ago. Their trade brought them beads and other items from ancient Mesopotamia, Rome and India, while Egyptian beads found here have been dated to around 200BC. They built stone walls, too, in the fashion of Great Zimbabwe, and the ruins of similar structures are to be seen to the east, at Dzata, in the former homeland Republic of Venda.

Intermittent warfare between the Venda people, who are descendants of 17th century migrants from Zimbabwe, and the Voortrekkers, led to the abandonment of Schoemansdal in 1867 and the people of the town retreated southwards, eventually to be granted building-plots in the town of Pietersburg, now the capital of the Northern Province.

It is from Pietersburg that a road leads east to the little village of Haenertsburg, once the centre of the defunct Woodbush Goldfields and now a starting point for the remote and lovely Wolkberg Wilderness Area. East of Haenertsburg the road plunges into the scenic Magoebaskloof, named for the Batlou chief Makgoba who, resisting republican Transvaal expansion, died somewhere on the slopes here in 1895 in defence of his people's right to live by the graves of their ancestors. No shades of unhappy things linger in this most scenic and densely wooded gorge, through which the road descends to Tzaneen, dropping some 600 metres in less than six kilometres. Water flashes lighthearted over the Debegeni Falls, and emerald tea plantations cover the rolling hills, while the still blue waters of vast dams stretch away in the distance.

The Wolkberg or 'cloud mountain' that lies close to Tzaneen is one of the northernmost outliers of the great Drakensberg range that runs south and west, its influence felt in five provinces of South Africa, as well as in the mountain kingdom of Lesotho, to end in the faraway Eastern Cape. Everywhere impressive, the Drakensberg is perhaps at its most awesome near the little town of Graskop. Here is the Mpumalanga Escarpment, where the mountain wall drops away almost sheer to the Lowveld, and distant views from such vantage points as God's Window or Wonderview extend far over the Kruger National Park to Mozambique.

Gold was found on the high ground – in the many waterfalls named Berlin, Lisbon, Bridal Veil, Sabie, Panorama and MacMac, in the Blyde and Treur rivers, and in Pilgrim's Creek. MacMac, it is said, was given its name by an amiable but ineffectual president of the old Transvaal republic, Thomas Burgers who, on a visit to the mining camp, found so many Scotsmen whose name started with 'Mac' that he declared the place should be named MacMac.

The most enduring gold strike in the area was made at Pilgrim's Rest, in 1874, and the little town – built mostly from corrugated iron – survives as a living memorial to those early days. They chose iron because it was cheaper than bricks and, being foreigners, the diggers expected almost any day to be ordered out of a country which had no love for *uitlanders* other than Hollanders. There are many tales of Pilgrim's Rest – of the stage coach being held up and robbed of gold, of a nameless robber's grave in the old cemetery, of the hotel bar that once was a Catholic chapel in Maputo, and many more. Time to explore the area is well spent, and it lies on the scenic Panorama Route that also takes in the Great Escarpment, waterfalls, the Blyde River Canyon and the strangely eroded potholes known as Bourke's Luck.

A short distance south of Pilgrim's Rest is the town of Sabie, once also the scene of frantic gold-seeking, but now surrounded by immense forest plantations. Sabie is linked to Lydenburg – once the capital of yet another early Boer republic – by the magnificently scenic Long Tom Pass, a smooth ribbon of road that winds and soars for close to 50 kilometres across the Drakensberg. From Sabie the road, often mist-shrouded in summer, rises some 1 000 metres to the summit, dropping again almost 700 metres to Lydenburg. This was the old 'harbour road', a strenuous wagon-route to the sea at Delagoa Bay in the days of the Zuid-Afrikaansche Republiek. Lack of ready access to a harbour was one of the republic's major concerns, and all efforts to expand its territory to the coastline were frustrated by Great Britain.

Long Tom was the name that British soldiers, and later the Boers themselves, gave to the four Creusot siege guns that the old republic purchased from France shortly before the outbreak of the Anglo-Boer War in 1899. The guns were manufactured to a design already 20 years old, and it seems likely that the ammunition supplied by France was of a similar vintage, as it frequently failed to explode at the right moment. In a fighting retreat after the last major pitched battle of the war, fought at Bergendal near Belfast in August 1900, the Boers manhandled two of these Long Tom guns across the rough mountain road, successfully engaging the pursuing British infantry at close range. A full-scale metal replica of a Long Tom stands stark and silent by the roadside – a sudden and surprising reminder of distant turmoil in this tranquil setting.

Another route down to the Lowveld in Kowyn's Pass, between Graskop at an altitude of 1 488 metres and Bosbokrand, some 500 metres lower. The road affords good views of the sheer, rocky buttresses of the escarpment as it winds at a gentle gradient to the wide, flat plains. The Lowveld proper reaches its highest altitude at around 650 metres above sea level, and is separated by the ridge of the Lebombo Mountains from the coastal plain of Mozambique. In the hot summers malaria is prevalent, and bilharzia is a danger in many areas, but on this plain of tall grasses and deciduous and evergreen trees are some of Africa's last kingdoms of the wild, of which the largest and best known is the Kruger National Park.

A lthough it is Paul Kruger, Afrikaner patriarch and president of the Zuid-Afrikaansche Republiek, who is honoured in the name of this world famous wildlife preserve, the Kruger National Park in its present form owes more to the efforts of other men, paramount among them being Colonel James Stevenson-Hamilton, a retired British army officer who became its first warden and doggedly fought for its survival against political and logistic odds that would have defeated a lesser man. Within the Park, however, there are constant reminders of the efforts of this indefatigable soldier

none more fitting, perhaps, than the Park's 'capital', the village-camp of Skukuza, the name given to Stevenson-Hamilton by his Shangaan staff and which means 'he who scrapes clean', a reference to his relentless war against poaching. Today, the Kruger National Park is the flagship of an expanding chain of national parks that are one of the prides of South Africa. Sometimes known as 'Africa's largest hotel', the Kruger Park has facilities that can cater for several thousand visitors daily, with accommodation ranging from rudimentary to luxurious.

Winter is probably the best season for game-viewing, when the grass is short and many of the trees have lost their leaves. This is also the dry season, when animals are easily spotted in the vicinity of water-holes, but a leisurely drive at any time of the year is sure to bring close sightings of game. For the more adventurous, there are regular hiking expeditions led by experienced rangers.

Along the western boundary of the Kruger National Park are a number of private game reserves, including Timbavati, Manyeleti and Sabi Sand, where guests are catered for in ultra-luxurious lodges and are introduced to the bush in open, four-wheel-drive vehicles.

Most visitors do not feel they have seen the real Africa until they have had a close-up look at a lion, the famed King of the Beasts. The English word for a group of lions – a pride – is a measure of the mystique and veneration accorded the lion. But despite all the fables, and its honoured place in heraldry, the lion seldom presents a very regal aspect. Most often to be seen resting in the shade, the lion allows his females to do most of the work of hunting, but insists on being the first to feed at a kill. An adult male may weigh as much as 220 kilograms, and a normal life span is around 20 years. The male lion is the only member of the cat family to carry a mane, the great ruff of hair on the crest of the neck, varying in colour from golden yellow to black. Contrary to popular belief, lions can (and do) climb trees, and are not at all afraid of water. Once roused, the lion is very fast indeed, and can cover 100 metres in around four seconds – less than half the time of a trained athlete. But stamina is lacking and any animal able to avoid the first rush is likely to escape.

Many people feel that the lion's noble title really belongs to the elephant, which once roamed the subcontinent but is now predominantly confined to reserves in Mpumalanga, northern KwaZulu-Natal and the Eastern Cape at Addo.

Largest land animal after the elephant is the white rhinoceros which, like the black rhinoceros, is actually a greyish colour. Solitary and aggressive, the black rhino is smaller than the white, and has a pointed, prehensile upper lip that it uses to grasp twigs while it is browsing. The white rhino, standing up to two metres high at the shoulder, has a wide, square lip, and is a grazer.

Also among the heavyweights, with a bull tipping the scale at 1 500 kilograms, is the hippopotamus which, for most of the year, shares its river-home amicably with the crocodile. However, crocodiles have been known to attack baby hippos, so when a cow is about to give birth, her companions chase away all crocodiles from the vicinity. With their thick skins very sensitive to heat and sunlight, hippo spend most of the day in water, and the cows actually suckle their calves under water, the calf surfacing every minute or so to take a breath. The hippo's massive jaws, equipped with fearsome teeth, can bite clean through a large crocodile with a single snap, but the hippo is purely a vegetarian, devouring up to 180 kilograms of grasses and reed shoots in a night.

Another large animal fond of wallowing is the buffalo, a gregarious species often seen in large herds, numbering hundreds. Like so many other African animals, buffalo were once widespread from the Cape Peninsula to the Limpopo River and beyond, but now their range is limited to the country's wildlife sanctuaries.

*T*he Highveld covers Gauteng, parts of the Northern and North-West provinces and all of the Free State with the exception of a length of its border with KwaZulu-Natal and Lesotho. Here, we encounter again the mighty Drakensberg range, as well as the Maluti mountains of Lesotho, where erosion of the sandstone in the foothills zone has produced the striking formations encompassed in the Golden Gate Highlands National Park. The Golden Gate itself consists of two massive 'headlands', while an even more spectacular feature is known as Brandwag, a formation that suggests to some the bows of a gigantic ocean liner protruding from the wall of a rock. Nestling nearby is the picturesque little town of Clarens, named after the Swiss town in which Paul Kruger, last president of the Zuid-Afrikaansche Republiek, died in exile in 1904. Born in 1825, Kruger took part as a boy in the Great Trek, including a battle against the Matabele at Vechtkop. Although their laager, so central to Boer military tactics, stayed intact, the Voortrekkers lost all their draught cattle to the Matabele and, afraid to venture far from their defences, they remained effectively besieged until eventually

A steam drawn passenger train puffs its way across the landscape. South Africa has one of the few remnant steam engine populations in the world and enthusiasts from all four corners make the pilgrimage to see these majestic old timers in action. The country's railway showpiece, however, the internationally acclaimed 'Blue Train' which plies twice weekly between Johannesburg and Cape Town, is, together with the great majority of contemporary passenger and goods rolling stock, drawn by diesel-electric power.

rescued by the friendly Baralong people. Many battles lay ahead of Kruger who, once he had become president, ruled his republic as a dictator, swaying his Volksraad (parliament) to do his bidding and dismissing his Chief Justice who questioned whether mere 'resolutions' of the Volksraad were, in fact, actually laws.

Kruger, regarded as 'backward' in Britain and by imperialists such as Cecil Rhodes, had a great love for his own people – the Boers – and for his country. With deep religious convictions rooted in the Old Testament, his arch-conservatism led to deep misgivings about the long-term effect of the gold discovery on the Witwatersrand and the many foreigners or *uitlanders* it attracted. His system of granting monopolies or concessions – for almost anything from the provision of water to Johannesburg, to the importation of dynamite – discouraged investment and the development of industry. *Uitlanders* had no vote, and blacks, taxed in an attempt to force them onto the labour market, had few rights.

Ironically, through the medium of Cape Governor Sir Alfred Milner, Kruger eventually did yield on most issues raised by Britain, such as citizenship or voting rights for *uitlanders*. As so often in South African history, however, it was a case of too little too late as the urgings of the mine magnates had already determined the British government to make the Zuid-Afrikaansche Republiek a British colony.

The war that broke out in October 1899 went well for the Boers at first, thanks largely to British military incompetence, but sheer numbers eventually prevailed. With his country overrun, Kruger was moved by rail eastwards, and finally sailed into exile on a warship sent by the sympathetic Queen of the Netherlands. Attempts to raise European assistance proved vain, and the long road that began with the Great Trek ended in a villa at Clarens, Switzerland.

The mountains around the South African Clarens were for long the home of the little people known as Bushmen, or San. These were hunter-gatherers, growing no crops and keeping no livestock, living in a harmony with the earth. Their weapon was the bow and arrow tipped with poison, and much of their culture remains subject to speculation, as is the interpretation of the many enduring rock-paintings they left as reminders of their passing. Many of the paintings are clearly of recognizable animals or people in various situations – hunting, at war, peacefully feeding. Other paintings are mysterious, and intrigued academics have sought to explain them in terms of a link between the spirit world and the real world, depictions of hallucinations that occurred to medicine-men in a state of trance. There is much to learn about San culture, but there is no mystery about their fate. Despised and feared as cattle rustlers, they were attacked by black pastoralists as well as by white settlers. Deliberately hunted down, they were eventually shot out of existence, to disappear forever from the mountains not only of the Free State, but all of South Africa. Remnant populations exist in neighbouring Botswana and Namibia, but acculturation has destroyed their 'way of life perfected'.

The provincial capital of the Free State, Bloemfontein, is the seat of South Africa's highest judicial authority, the Court of Appeal. The city has a number of buildings of architectural interest, including the charming little building, dating back to 1849, in which the Boer republic's first Volksraad (parliament) sat to deliberate their country's future. Bloemfontein is also the site of the War Museum of the Boer Republics, an institution that will provide the curious visitor with an excellent background to the Afrikaner's own 'freedom struggle'. Loyal to its sister republic, the old Oranje Vrij-Staat also went to war against Britain in 1899, and suffered immense damage as a result. A feature of this Anglo-Boer War was the establishment by the British of concentration camps for civilian Boers at points where it would be convenient for the British Army to supply them with food and water.

The need to concentrate civilians at all arose out of the British strategy of destroying Boer farmsteads and livestock to deprive the Boers, in the guerilla phase of the war, of the means to replenish themselves. However, the British army was unable to care adequately even for the health of its own soldiers, and proved hopelessly incapable of shouldering this new burden. How many Boer women and children would have died if left alone to fend for themselves on the veld, cannot be estimated, but the horrifying total of 26 000 died in the camps.

*T*here is an interesting memorial near the top of one of the old Drakensberg passes by which parties of Voortrekkers descended to KwaZulu-Natal where, in due course, another republic was created. Earlier, a group of Voortrekker men had gone ahead to meet and negotiate for land with King Dingane of the Zulus. One of these was Pieter Retief, formerly an unsuccessful builder who was eventually to be regarded as the principal martyr of the Great Trek. While he was away his daughter painted his name and the date – his birthday – on a sheltered rock at the feature called Kerkenberg, or 'church mountain'. The site commands breathtaking views, looking over the 'garden province' of KwaZulu-Natal.

The ubiquitous windmill (above) creaks and groans on almost every farm across the vast central plateau of South Africa. Irregular rainfall and often prolonged and severe periods of drought are the plague of the country's agricultural industry. Very often the only source of water for man, beast and crops is from subterranean resources pumped by windmills from considerable depths.

Sunflowers (*Helianthus annuus*) (left) are also characteristic of the inland landscape where fields often seem to stretch to the very horizon. Sunflower seeds are rich in oil and are widely used in the manufacture of margarine and cooking oils, the demand for which has soared in concert with the world trend away from animal fats.

The provincial capital is Pietermaritzburg, an amalgamation of the names of Voortrekker leaders Pieter Retief and Gerrit Maritz, and often known by the abbreviated form of Maritzburg. This small but busy city is softened by the greenery of parks and the mellowness of Victorian red-brick buildings. Downtown Maritzburg is dominated by the imposing City Hall, completed in 1900 and said to be the largest all-brick building in the southern hemisphere. There are many other relics of the heady days of colonialism and there is even a relic, ephemeral though it may be, of the French Second Empire: a hitching rail outside the Imperial Hotel to which the young Prince Imperial of France tied the reins of his horse for a day or two in 1879. The prince was present as an observer with the British army then invading Zululand. On a patrol through country supposedly cleared of the enemy, the prince fell beneath Zulu assegaais when his companions fled an ambush. And so, in a remote corner of Africa, was written the end to a great European dynasty.

The war of 1879 against the Zulu people was one of the less glorious interludes, both morally and militarily, of British imperialism. Under pressure from the Transvaal on one hand, and colonial Natal on the other, the Zulu kingdom was understandably in a state of tension which communicated itself to the Natal settlers, who demanded a 'solution'. War was engineered by making huge demands of the Zulu king, Cetshwayo, and then, when the demands were not entirely met, sending three columns of British and colonial troops to invade Zululand. At Isandlwana the Zulus, armed only with spears and clubs, inflicted the most shattering defeat ever suffered by soldiers armed with breech-loading rifles. On the British side, some 800 white soldiers and 470 black auxiliaries died, and the Zulu loss was also grievously high.

The Zulus can justifiably lay claim to being one of the most famous of Africa's peoples. Yet less than two centuries ago they were a relatively insignificant clan in the rolling hills of the subtropical eastern hinterland. And they would probably have remained thus had it not been for the military genius of one of their sons, Shaka. In the space of little more than a decade this strong, ruthless and quick-minded warrior welded the surrounding clans into a fighting machine that conquered, annihilated or incorporated all before them in a *blitzkrieg* that changed the course of African history. Starving refugees fled across the high Drakensberg and fell upon the people of the high plains who in turn fled and pillaged to survive, giving impetus to a chain reaction that coursed across the southern continent. During this ghastly period known by the name of *difaqane*, or 'crushing', countless thousands must have died, but new nations also came into being: the Matabele who under Mzilikazi, himself a renegade general of Shaka's, became a force of formidable strength and which all but ended the Voortrekkers' dream of a promised land before it had begun; and the Basotho, forged from refugees who took to the relative safety of the high country by the resourceful Moshweshwe, whose mountain kingdom of Lesotho remains fiercely independent to this day.

Shaka had no children, but his family and their successive offspring have ruled the Zulu people to the present, from Shaka's half-brother Dingane to the present King Goodwill Zwelethini. But the present monarch sits an uncomfortable throne, with most of the real political power being held by the charismatic Mangosuthu Buthelezi, South African cabinet minister and himself of royal blood, his great-grandfather being Cetshwayo who humiliated the British at Isandlwana.

*I*t is not far from Pietermaritzburg to the resorts and reserves of the Drakensberg, strung like a garland along the high border with Lesotho. The Drakensberg range – often referred to simply as The Berg – is perhaps at its most scenically splendid in KwaZulu-Natal, where peaks that are grassy green in summer, shimmer with snow and ice in the months of winter. A great many trails await exploration on foot or on horseback, and accommodation ranges from luxury hotels and cosy cottages to somewhat spartan huts and caves. In these rocky fastnesses, the Bushmen made their home, and left their painted records on the rocks. Rock paintings in southern Africa have been scientifically dated to 26 000 years before the present. Close to the camp in Giant's Castle Game Reserve are caves where a Bushman Site Museum has been developed amid hundreds of rock paintings. Battle Cave, above the nearby Injasuti River, is named for the theme of some of the many paintings that decorate its walls, and houses another site museum. Battles have been such a feature of KwaZulu-Natal history that there is even a Battlefields Route in the province, followed by many military enthusiasts every year. It takes in battles fought by the Voortrekkers, of which Blood River is the principal site, the Anglo-Zulu war of 1879, the Anglo-Transvaal war of 1880-1881, and the Anglo-Boer War of 1899-1902.

Riding the roller-coaster freeway that threads the KwaZulu-Natal coast with its hinterland, the serene, orderly farmlands that stretch far to each side make the turmoils of the past seem like an historic interlude. But the reality is tragically different, for the battle rages on deep in the rural areas, hidden from the eye of the casual traveller. Here in the villages, townships and countryside the ongoing violence is far more complex than that of aspirant black nationals skirmishing with the white establishment. Here in an awful morass of confusion, age-old feuds between rival Zulu factions persist and are fanned by poverty, unemployment and the macro-political power-struggle between followers of Chief Buthelezi's Inkatha Freedom Party and the African National Congress.

*F*ar northern KwaZulu-Natal is an uneasy mix of rural settlements, agriculture, timber plantations, mining industries and natural wilderness of some 9 000 square kilometres in the transition zone between tropics and sub-tropics. Here are the Tembe and Ndumo game reserves, which, together with the Greater St Lucia Wetland Park and the Sodwana Bay National Park, make up the region known as Maputaland.

St Lucia, a series of shallow lakes, of dunes and white, sandy beaches, is home to crocodile and hippopotamus and a host of waterbirds. Beaches within the reserve are the breeding grounds of the loggerhead and leatherback turtles. The leatherback, largest of the marine turtles, is also the most powerful and fastest swimmer of the turtle family, and may attain a length of two metres and a weight in excess of 500 kilograms. Game fishing is popular in the offshore waters of the Maputaland coast, with Sodwana Bay being something of a mecca for the sport.

The coastal plains further south are covered with vast expanses of shiny green sugar cane, first grown here commercially in about 1850. Commercial cultivation, however, required a great amount of cheap labour in order to be adequately profitable, but the local Zulus saw no attraction in toiling in the fields to enrich white settlers.

In 1859, when a shortage of labour threatened to wreck Natal's economy, the colonial legislature voted to introduce labourers from India 'at public expense'. The contract or indenture, which most of the new labourers could not read, provided that each Indian would be assigned to a sugar planter for three years, and then re-assigned, perhaps to the same planter, for a further two years.

After five more years as a 'free' worker, each labourer would have the choice of returning to India on a free passage, or of remaining in Natal on a small grant of land.

Later, those who chose to stay on in Natal were subject to a punitive poll tax. India was in the throes of recovering from a bloody rebellion against British administration, and emigration, even to Natal and with the prospect of only the most meagre wages, seemed more attractive than staying.

Reports of harsh treatment and increasingly legislated discrimination caused the Indian government to halt the emigration of labourers in 1871. It was resumed a few years later, and continued until halted by the Indian government, this time permanently, in 1911, by which time about 150 000 Indians had entered Natal.

When Mohandes K Gandhi, later to be known as the Mahatma, or 'great soul', came to Natal in 1893 he was harshly introduced to the realities of discrimination in southern Africa. Despite having bought a first-class rail ticket, he was ejected from the first-class carriage and spent a night on Pietermaritzburg station. The scene has been immortalized in Sir Richard Attenborough's classic film epic on the Mahatma's life.

Having opened his own law practice in Durban, Gandhi founded the Natal Indian Congress to oppose laws restricting Indian settlement, not only in the colony of Natal, but also in the republican Transvaal. Only after his actions, for which he and many followers were imprisoned on occasion, had brought into being the Indians' Relief Act of 1914, did Gandhi return to India.

Durban is Africa's principal harbour, an important industrial centre and South Africa's major holiday resort. The climate is subtropical, and the warm waters of the Indian Ocean lap the sands of a city that is a unique blend of the life-styles of Africa, Asia and Europe. Bathing beaches, well protected by anti-shark nets, stretch for some four kilometres from Addington Beach in the south, to Country Club and Blue Lagoon.

The area of Marine Parade abuts the beachfront and during weekends and holiday seasons throngs with visitors to the aquarium, dolphinarium and snake park, the fun fair and aerial cableway.

The Botanic Gardens boasts an orchid house that is a blaze of springtime colour, and the green open spaces include Jameson Park, known for its more than 200 rose varieties.

The beachfront can be and often is a vibrant place, fringed by hotel and apartment block after hotel and apartment block, some smart and glitzy and others, especially those just off the 'Golden Mile', on the seedy side and the meeting place of Durban's other world of prostitution and drugs.

Aspirant musicians listen to the master at work (above). Abdullah Ibrahim, one of South Africa's leading jazz musicians, is once again captivating his local fans after years of self-imposed exile.

outh of Durban the highway runs slightly inland through lush, green fields, while the old coast road stays closer to the seemingly endless succession of beaches that make this an extension of the 'holiday city'. The main road swings inland at Port Shepstone (which, although it retains that name, is no longer a port) and passes close to scenic Oribi Gorge. Here, over millions of years, the waters of the Mzimkulwana River have etched a 24 kilometre ravine deep into the layered sandstone. At the heart of the gorge lies a large nature reserve.

Beyond the southern border of KwaZulu-Natal lies the region known for more than a century as Transkei. Until 1994, it was another of the independent homeland republics. The name means 'beyond the Kei (River)' – when viewed from the old-time seat of administration, Cape Town. This has been the home for centuries of groups of Nguni people who speak dialects of the language *isiXhosa*, characterized by a large number of 'click' consonants – a linguistic inheritance from contact with Bushman languages. It was with the long-settled Xhosa peoples that the expanding Cape settlement clashed in 1779, and wars on the shifting frontier of the colony, first against the Dutch and later the British, continued sporadically for 100 years.

Although still commonly referred to as Transkei, the area has been formally incorporated into South Africa as part of the Eastern Cape Province. It is principally an agricultural region, although former government incentives to 'border industries' have led to the establishment of an industrial base. The regional economy has also been boosted by a considerable amount of capital invested by Taiwanese enterprise. Other income is derived, traditionally, from the wages earned by migrant workers, from tourism and hotels (including casinos) and, for many years, immense sums pumped in by a South African government anxious that its partitionist schemes should appear workable.

Much of this part of the Eastern Cape consists of rolling, grassy hills, the rounded summits often crowned with a group of homesteads, with most of the doorways facing east.

The traditional reed dwellings of the rural areas have given way to circular homes of mud or bricks-and-mortar and, increasingly, to houses that have a rectangular floor-plan. Several large rivers have cut deep into the countryside and, in many places, soil erosion is a serious problem, the inevitable result of over-use of the land. For here, as in so many parts of rural South Africa, overpopulation and lack of opportunity, exacerbated during 'grand apartheid' by the forced return of thousands of dispossessed people, has resulted in abject poverty.

Despite these open wounds the region has its beauty, with perhaps the loveliest part being its coastline, known between the mouths of the Umtamvuna and Kei rivers as the Wild Coast, a paradise for anglers and hikers. Long stretches of beach are intersected by the mouths of some 18 rivers, some of which form tranquil, shallow lagoons. Holiday resorts and nature reserves are dotted along the coast, each with its own particular character.

Southwards from the west bank of the Kei, the coast changes its character, becoming a long succession of gleaming beaches and lagoons interrupted with grassy hills and headlands. The principal town of the area is East London which, with its varied surrounds, has many attractions that deserve to be better known. To the west of East London lies another of the former independent homeland republics, Ciskei, which, like Transkei, now also forms part of the Eastern Cape Province. Bisho, previously the capital of Ciskei, is now the capital of the new province. The 'Border', as the area between the former republics was known, was for many years the frontier of the old Cape Colony, which progressively shifted its boundary eastward. The greatest scenic attractions inland are probably the Hogsback and the Katberg area, both of them boasting resorts amid cool forests, waterfalls and superb mountain scenery.

Benevolent European intrusion, as opposed to wars and cattle-raids, came fairly early to what was then known as Ciskei with the establishment of a mission near the town of Alice. Here was founded the Lovedale Institution in the 1820s, where Scottish missionaries preached the Gospel and taught young black men 'useful trades'.

In time, academic education was introduced and this, in turn, brought the need for tertiary education. The South African Native College was officially founded in 1915, on the site of Fort Hare on the outskirts of Alice. From being affiliated to Rhodes University in Grahamstown it has emerged as a fully fledged university, numbering among its graduates many leaders from within South Africa and beyond. Among the distinguished alumni are leaders of the African National Congress, including the State President, Nelson Mandela, while Archbishop Desmond Tutu served for a while as the university's chaplain.

Historically, Ciskei dates back to a quarrel within the ruling Gcaleka Xhosa family in the 18th century, resulting in one faction crossing the Kei to settle in the south.

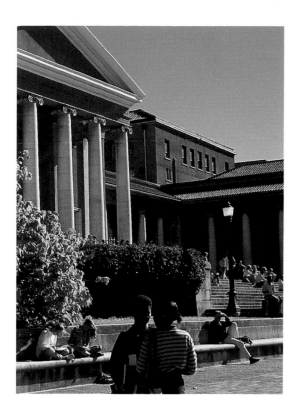

The University of Cape Town (above) is one of South Africa's leading seats of learning. The main campus sprawls across the eastern slopes of Devil's Peak, which flanks Table Mountain, providing what must be the most spectacular setting of any university anywhere in the world. Education, even the basic skills of reading and writing (left, above), is one of the greatest challenges that face the present and future leaders of the country.

The border with the old Cape Colony was a troubled one, much disputed by the people on both sides of it. In a cynical attempt to introduce some stability and, as important, to reduce expenditure on military garrisons, the British government sponsored the emigration of some 4 000 settlers from the British Isles in 1820. These were granted farming allotments along the frontier and were expected to be self-sufficient within a short time, although only very few had had any farming experience, and none was familiar with local conditions. Many were unequal to the challenge and abandoned their lands, returning to their old trades in the towns.

For those who claim descent from the settlers of 1820, their spiritual 'home' is Grahamstown, which lies more or less at the centre of the area allotted their ancestors. Known as the City of Saints, from its many churches, Grahamstown is also the home of Rhodes University and a number of highly regarded schools. It is also home to the 1820 Settlers National Monument which has inevitably been compared with the Voortrekker Monument in Pretoria. The essential difference, though, is that the Settlers Monument, on Gunfire Hill, was designed not so much as a shrine or museum, but as a practical conference centre, and to the credit of its trustees has for many years hosted the National Festival of the Arts which increasingly reflects the richness and power of a South African culture transcending the divisions of the past.

The British settlers were landed on the sandy shores of Algoa Bay, under the guns of Fort Frederick. As commerce and industry developed in the interior, the need for a safe harbour became apparent. Algoa Bay became the site of ambitious construction that has resulted in the sprawling harbour city and seaside resort of Port Elizabeth.

A port that failed to survive as a viable commercial harbour is Knysna, situated around a natural lagoon in a stretch of Cape coast that, from its great natural beauty, is known as the Garden Route. There are no official boundaries to the Garden Route, but it is usually accepted as being the coastal plateau traversed by the N2 national road between Humansdorp (west of Port Elizabeth) and the little town of Swellendam which, in the 18th century, set a much-followed South African precedent by declaring its independence.

The Garden Route includes the largest area of surviving indigenous forest in South Africa, where giant yellowwood trees reach an age beyond a thousand years and heights of up to 60 metres. The coastline is an idyllic mix of rocky cliffs, long stretches of sandy beach, quiet lagoons and navigable river estuaries. Tsitsikamma National Park protects both the shoreline and the sea itself, as well as a stretch of fine indigenous forest. The Garden Route is a place of gentle pleasures, fishing, quiet boating along the protected inland waterways, exploring the craft shops and history of the towns or riding the vintage, steam-powered narrow-gauge railway routes. But above all the Garden Route is walking country, for opportunities abound from gentle day walks in shaded woodland to taxing four to five day hikes, the most famous of which is the Otter Trail, which follows the rugged coastline from the Tsitsikamma National Park to Nature's Valley.

Plettenberg Bay towards the Garden Route's eastern limit is known throughout South Africa and beyond as a beautiful playground for the wealthy. It was on this lovely beach that South Africa's first (unintended) European settlement came into being in 1630 when survivors of a Portuguese shipwreck set up camp. They built two small boats and, eventually, sailed away. Most property owners at 'Plett' are also temporary sojourners, and magnificent dwellings stand empty for most of the year, the permanent population being relatively small.

Knysna – nobody is really sure what the name means – may have failed as a port, but it remains one of the prettiest towns in all South Africa, situated on a wide-spreading lagoon that enters the sea through a gateway of massive stone cliffs known as The Heads. Founded almost two centuries ago by the enigmatically named George Rex, a supposed morganatic son of England's King George II, Knysna is maintained on forestry and associated industry, and tourism. At about the time the Witwatersrand goldfields were opened, men were toiling for gold, and finding it, in the forest at nearby Millwood. Fortunately for the serene beauty of the Garden Route, Millwood's gold gave out and Knysna did not, as had been anticipated, become 'the port of South Africa'.

The Garden Route is a region of immense environmental importance, but its ever-growing popularity is also its Achilles' heel as more and more real estate development takes place. Large tracts of forest and the coast have for many years been protected by the National Parks Act, but until recently the lakes area between Knysna and the larger town of George to the west were not so. These salt and freshwater wetland areas are especially fragile and are depended upon by a complex web of plant and animal life. Fortunately, these ecosystems now form part of two conservation areas, the Wilderness National Park and the Knysna National Lakes Area.

Westwards, beyond George lies Mossel Bay, where Portuguese explorers first set foot on our southern shores in 1488. Today it is a fishing harbour and the land terminal for off-shore oil drilling operations. From here and from George, scenic passes lead inland over the Outeniqua Mountains into the long, narrow plain called the Langkloof, part of the Little Karoo which is bounded to the north by the mighty Swartberg range. This is the land of the ostrich, especially around the town of Oudtshoorn, where fortunes were made out of prime feathers, which became the country's most important export after gold, wool and diamonds. The market collapsed early in 1914, but a number of baronial 'ostrich palaces' are still to be seen, and show farms operate in the district. Oudtshoorn is also famous for its Cango Caves, a series of connected limestone caverns believed to be the most extensive in the world.

*B*eyond the Swartberg – the black mountains – lies the immense and arid plain of the Great Karoo, its name derived from a word meaning 'dry' or 'bare' in the language of the vanished people known as Khoikhoi. The Great Karoo covers some 400 000 square kilometres of the Cape provinces as well as parts of the Free State, or about one third of the land surface of South Africa. It is a vast area of low rainfall, of searingly hot summer days and freezing winter nights. Ironically, when rains do come they may occur as floods, such as the deluge that all but destroyed the town of Laingsburg in 1981. Vegetation consists mainly of hardy succulents that survive by storing water in their thick, fleshy leaves. In some parts, though, there are brief moments of floral glory, lasting no more than a few weeks in springtime, and then only if there has been adequate rain in winter.

To see the usually barren landscape literally carpeted with colourful, ephemeral blossoms is an unforgettable experience. Sheep-farming is the principal rural occupation of the Karoo, and the wants of scattered communities are provided for by numerous small towns – the typical 'dorps' of South Africa – as well as by the larger centres such as Beaufort West and Graaff-Reinet.

Barren though it may appear to the traveller passing through by car (or, perhaps, aboard the luxurious Blue Train that sweeps silently and effortlessly between Johannesburg and Cape Town), the Great Karoo does indeed sustain its own pattern of life. In prehistoric times it was an area of swampy forest; innumerable fossils testify to the existence of dinosaurs both great and small, and the subsequent group of mammal-like reptiles. In more recent times the Great Karoo supported herds of springbok, Cape mountain zebra, red hartebeest and gemsbok among others, but these were either shot or simply could not compete for grazing with the domestic herds introduced by settlers.

In the far north there is the Kalahari Gemsbok National Park, a great tongue of land between Namibia and Botswana. At 960 000 hectares it is roughly half the size of the Kruger Park, and home not only to the sabre-horned gemsbok, but to lion, cheetah, leopard, eland and several smaller antelope, as well as to 200 bird species. This is the furthermost corner of the Northern Cape, beyond the Diamond City of Kimberley where the Big Hole remains the largest and deepest excavation ever carried out by man-power alone.

Over 43 years men toiled to remove around 25 million tons of earth from which three tons of diamonds were recovered and by which time the original hillock of Colesberg koppie had disappeared. In its place was a hole 365 metres deep and with a mean diameter of about 460 metres. Close to the rim of this great mine, which is no longer worked, is the Open Air Mine Museum, a re-creation of old Kimberley.

Kimberley lies close to the Vaal River, where the gravels have yielded their burden of diamonds, and where the bright stones are still sought and found. Not far to the southwest of Kimberley the Vaal joins the Orange River, named not for its colour but in honour of the Netherlands royal house of Orange. It is still often spoken of as 'Grootrivier' – the big river – and it flows west through arid country, especially ironic in the vicinity of Augrabies where, encased in its channel of deeply incised granite, the river yields nothing to the parched lands around its course.

It is at Augrabies, in desert country, that the river makes a sudden plunge of 56 metres over a rocky rim into a mysterious, troubled pool believed to be 130 metres deep. The falls are the central feature of the Augrabies Falls National Park, which includes the eroded granite chasm that the river has carved for itself, sometimes to a depth of 250 metres, over a length of 15 kilometres.

The Orange River flows on to become the border between South Africa and Namibia, reaching the cold Atlantic where, on the beaches, huge machines remove sand overburden to expose bedrock in the unending search for alluvial diamonds. South of the river lies the pitilessly dry mountain zone of the Richtersveld.

The pub sign at the Greyton Lodge
(left) which nestles in the Riviersonderend mountains in the Western Cape. The lodge is one of the many country house hotels where superior cuisine and first-class accommodation are combined with the peace and tranquility of a rural hideaway.

The wildflowers of Namaqualand
(below) carpet the veld in all the colours of the rainbow for a short few weeks in spring, but only if the preceding winter rains have been good.

At Steinkopf are still to be seen huts built to the ancient, traditional pattern of the Nama, although sacking forms a more convenient cover than the reeds of bygone times. This is the northern fringe of the part of Namaqualand renowned for its dramatic floral transformation for just a few weeks in spring. For the rest of the year the landscape is one of dry and sandy wastes, with great granite boulders stained green through the action of copper salts. But with spring, a rich carpet of blooms appears almost overnight, to cover all harshness in a brief blaze of triumphant colour.

Along the Namaqualand coast, where nightly sea mists drift inland to provide the only source of water to the hardy vegetation of the region, small fishing villages have developed to harvest the bountiful cold currents sweeping north from Antartica. Boats still put to sea with nets, but many carry divers and suction pipes to exploit the diamonds that litter the sea floor. Port Nolloth, Hondeklipbaai, Strandfontein and Doringbaai, Elands Bay and Lambert's Bay, each has a mystique and fund of tales and legends all its own.

Fishing boats put out, too, from villages along the wide sweep of St Helena Bay, from Paternoster where the lighthouse beam from Cape Columbine warns of treacherous reefs, and from Saldanha Bay at the head of the shallow and lovely Langebaan lagoon. History has it that the 17th century Dutch settlement at Table Bay would have been made here at Saldanha, on the shores of the natural, sheltered harbour, if only a reliable source of fresh water had been available. Iron ore from dry, faraway Sishen is shipped out in huge bulk carriers from the bay that once echoed to the cannon-fire of British and Dutch ships of the line and, in the 1860s, sheltered the elegant Confederate ship *Alabama*, a commerce raider that preyed on the laden ships of the Yankee north. Today all is peace, and Langebaan lagoon lies at the heart of the West Coast National Park renowned for its remarkable birdlife, including the Arctic tern and many other avian migrants.

*T*he Dutch settlement at Table Bay came in the year 1652, and its purpose was to provide fresh fruit, vegetables and meat to the fleets of the powerful United Dutch East Company on their long voyages between Europe and the East. Cattle, at first, were bartered from the local Khoikhoi, whom European callers referred to as Hottentots, the end result of this new commercial influence being total disruption of the old established trading patterns and, eventually, with the advent of diseases such as smallpox, the ruin and extinction of the Khoikhoi.

As the Khoikhoi declined, however, the new white settlement grew, slowly and uncertainly at first. The garden that provided poorly nourished seamen with fresh fruits exists to this day, although now as a botanical garden – known still as The Company's Gardens – at the heart of old Cape Town. The Castle of Good Hope dates from the 1680s and, although nominally still a military headquarters, houses many military and cultural exhibits and has been the subject of intensive archaeological work and reconstruction. The sea that once lapped at its bastions has been pushed far back by land recovery schemes that have created the city's sprawling foreshore, where great activity centres around the mid-19th century harbour area of the Victoria and Alfred Waterfront. Trawlers and tugboats come and go about their business as visitors relax at pubs or eating-houses, or explore the corners of a real working harbour. A maritime museum includes two floating exhibits, and plans are advanced for extending the waterfront scheme to re-unite the city with the sea and so bring back the days when Cape Town was known as 'the Tavern of the Seas'.

Cape Town, for all its splendid and dramatic setting below the steep crags of Table Mountain, has too often been careless of its heritage and allowed inappropriate buildings and roadways to mar its landscape. Its citizens protested vigorously against the construction of the upper cableway station at the top of their mountain, but since its opening in 1929 the cableway has been the city's most famous tourist amenity. Certainly, the view from the summit is unsurpassed, taking in the mountain-ous spine of the Cape Peninsula stretching away to the south, and the west coast of Africa beyond the curve of Table Bay with low-lying Robben Island. The island has a long and sad history as a prison, leper colony and insane asylum, fortress and a prison again. The name Robben Island is known throughout the world as the place where Nelson Mandela and his colleagues were imprisoned for so many long years. The island will always be a painful reminder of South Africa's slow and agonizing emancipation. In 1997, its days as a prison came to an end and Robben Island became a museum and nature reserve. Guided tours give visitors a glimpse of life on this windswept place of confinement.

An area of Cape Town that has changed little over more than a century and a half, lies on the slopes of Signal Hill and is known as Bo-Kaap. This is the traditional home of the Cape Muslims, often and erroneously called Cape Malays, just as Bo-Kaap was wrongly called 'the Malay quarter'. The Cape Muslims are a community united by the faith of Islam, and are largely descended from slaves and free blacks who were brought to the settlement from India and the East Indies to supply labour from the very earliest years. In addition, many learned men and people of noble birth who were troublesome to Dutch interests in the East were banished to the Cape settlement, and their descendants are here still. Mosques lend a touch of the East to narrow, cobbled streets lined by houses with neat Georgian facades. There are old buildings in the city that reflect colonial architecture at different stages of its development. Strand Street has its examples of 18th century domestic design, in Koopmans de Wet House, and of the ecclesiastical in the Lutheran Church complex. The Cultural History Museum developed under British rule from the old slave lodge and, on the Parliament Street facade, carries the most dejected lion and unicorn to be seen in any former British possession. The same sculptor, presumably under closer and indignant supervision, gave them their due heraldic dignity on the facade of the old Customs House in the Buitenkant, a street that once marked the town limits.

Cape Town, in the early years of settlement, saw the creation of a new people who came to be known as 'Cape coloured', and who were the offspring of liaisons and marriages between European settlers and slaves, or settlers and the indigenous peoples of South Africa. A law of the apartheid era made such sexual relationships a crime, and forbade the marriage of a European to a 'non-European'. Further legislation, concerned with where people of different colours might live, uprooted many communities – virtually all of them 'non-European'. Cape Town still bears the physical, commercial and psychological scars of this practice.

Tracts of empty land close to the city's heart were once closely settled, a near-slum where Victorian houses gone to seed jostled one another on narrow pavements in the predominantly coloured area known as District Six. Government edict proclaimed the area 'white', and residents of long standing were moved, against their will, to characterless settlements on the wide and windy Cape Flats. Their homes were broken down and the District's most famous thoroughfare, Hanover Street, was obliterated and replaced by a wide and sterile motor road called, with the most tenuous historical justification, Keisersgracht. Lots of land were put up for sale, but such was the shame and the stigma that few found buyers. Much interest now centres around the redevelopment of District Six in a non-racial South Africa. From the air, the apparently featureless ground still shows the ghosts of vanished roads and lanes trodden by people who are no longer living here. But redevelopment has begun as the modern buildings of the Cape Technikon start to encroach down towards the city.

An aerial trip, particularly by helicopter flight that can be arranged at the Waterfront, is an excellent way of seeing the Peninsula, and appreciating some of its scenery and some of its problems. Moving away from Table Bay and down the Atlantic seaboard is the cosmopolitan, high-rise and high-density suburb of Sea Point, squeezed, like Bantry Bay, Clifton and other seaside suburbs, between the shore and the mountain slopes. A deep indentation with an attractive harbour, used by commercial and leisure craft, is Hout Bay, from where rises one of the world's most scenic coastal highways. Chapman's Peak Drive clings close to the mountainside, soaring high above breakers that gnash at the base of the granite cliffs.

The most southerly part of the Peninsula is occupied by the Cape of Good Hope Nature Reserve, within which lies Cape Point. Tradition, rather than science, claims Cape Point to be the meeting place of the cold Atlantic and warm Indian oceans.

Flying up the False Bay coast it is again apparent how the proximity of sea and mountain dictate the extent of residential spread, from the naval port of Simon's Town to Fish Hoek. From Fish Hoek a low-lying, sandy plain extends to the west coast of the Peninsula and, in prehistoric times, seas that flowed through here made an island of the land to the south. Again, from Fish Hoek to Muizenberg, buildings are cramped between beach and berg.

A quick detour here along the long lines of surf rolling shoreward brings the astonishing sight of an immense sprawling settlement that has sprung up in the white, sandy dunes. It is a settlement of a kind that few people will have seen before, in which the houses are built of cardboard and plastic sheet, of sacking and newspaper, old iron and any material that can serve to provide some shelter from sun, wind and rain. These are some of the homeless, officially called squatters, who have travelled from areas of rural poverty in the hope of finding a better life in or near the city. Elsewhere in South Africa the problem of overcrowding and lack of even the vestiges of a good quality of life may not be as visible, but here at the Cape, which along with Durban has one of the highest rates of population growth of any conurbation in the world, they are painfully so, especially to those who travel regularly by air, as the flight path into what is undoubtedly one of the most beautiful cities in the world, takes one directly over these desperate areas. Although exacerbated by the apartheid laws now gone, such squatter settlements are not unique to South Africa and are all too common in the underdeveloped countries of the southern hemisphere. The only way out of this seemingly hopeless mess is through education and sustained economic growth at a rate unprecedented in South African history.

Brenda Fassie (above), one of South Africa's leading rock stars, belts it out for her fans.

Two players at the National Festival of the Arts (left above) which is held each year in the university city of Grahamstown in the Eastern Cape. Over the years the Festival, which embraces both the performing arts and the fine arts, has become a forum for the expression of aspirant and established performers alike.

Carnival time (left below). On the second day of January each year minstrel troupes in colourful silks and satins take to the streets of Cape Town in loud and cheerful celebration of the New Year.

Returning along the surf line and swinging inland, the vineyards of Constantia soon come into view, and the contrast is all the more telling for the previous experience. Here rows of stately oak trees line the avenues that lead to Groot Constantia, which lives on as a wine farm, its stately, gabled homestead just one of several Cape Peninsula examples of 18th century elegance and privilege. The modern suburbs of Constantia and adjoining Bishopscourt reflect the 20th century version, around the glorious garden that is Kirstenbosch. This is the headquarters of South Africa's National Botanic Gardens, established in 1913 on land bequeathed to the nation over a decade earlier by Cecil John Rhodes. At its most colourful in springtime, Kirstenbosch offers much at any time of the year, and has a cultivated section as well as a large area of natural veld renowned for the sparkling silver trees (*Leucadendron argenteum*) whose habitat range is confined almost exclusively to the Peninsula's mountain slopes. Although it is not true that the silver tree will die if it cannot 'see' Table Mountain, it is very difficult to grow elsewhere. A few survive on the mountainside near Stellenbosch.

*T*he towns of Stellenbosch, Paarl and Franschhoek, none of them more than an hour's drive from Cape Town, are at the heart of the wine-producing country, in valleys surrounded by steep, rugged mountains where vines bear their luscious crops in late summer. The wine industry in South Africa is a very old one, going back to the 1650s, although the quality of the product has improved beyond recognition since the early days, and South African wines have been accorded high honours at prestigious shows in many parts of the world. Each of the districts has its own wine route that one can follow from farm to farm, tasting the products of each, perhaps discussing them with the wine-maker. Harvest time is an ideal time to visit the wine farms, when the air is redolent of fermenting grapes, and loads of the grapes are busily brought in from the vineyards. Stellenbosch is the country's oldest European settlement after Cape Town, and was founded by Commander Simon van der Stel, not as a town, but as a farming community, in 1679. The town developed a few years later, and preserves the feel of early days in the Village Museum. Van der Stel, who urged his colonists to plant oaks, would be gratified by his town today, and a walk along oak-lined Dorp Street, with its enchanting old houses running the range from classic Cape Dutch to late Victorian, is one of the delights of Stellenbosch.

Nearby Paarl – 'the pearl' – was named by an explorer who, early one morning, caught a distant view of the great granite dome glistening with dew and named it 'the mountain of diamonds and pearls'. The long Main Street gives more than a glimpse of the town's old-world charm, with vineyards running right up to its verge, and thriving old farms snugly situated well within the residential area that, over the centuries, developed around them.

Franschhoek was named after the Huguenot refugees from religious persecution who were settled here in 1688. Preference was given to those who had some knowledge of viticulture and brandy-making but, in the event, few of them had such knowledge. The Huguenot Museum at Franschhoek has, apart from other exhibits, detailed genealogical records of these French pioneers, their ancestors and descendants. Farm names like Champagne, La Provence and La Dauphine, and many South African surnames, some of them Afrikanerized, are enduring memorials to the Huguenots.

On many of the wine farms, old homesteads still stand proud, and rest mellow and gracious in their settings of vine, oak and mountain. The Cape soon developed its own architectural traditions, based on those of the Netherlands and influenced in time by French Baroque and Rococo. The typical front facade shows windows symmetrically placed with a central front door beneath an ornate gable that is often the crowning glory of such houses. Entranced by the cool beauty of white walls and golden thatch, few people realize that the greater part of the labour and skill that went into creating these enduring monuments was probably that of slaves. Despite their bondage, the works they created may have brought them some relief and pleasure, in achievements that are appreciated still. With the passing of the old order in South Africa, and its many inequities, it is hoped that the good, and beautiful, will endure, as it must, if not for sentimental or aesthetic reasons, then simply for profit, for it is South Africa's supreme physical beauty, its bountiful wildlife, its botanical diversity, its history and broad cultural achievements, wherein lie its future success as a world tourist venue.

A forest glade (right) high in Magoebaskloof in the Northern Province's Drakensberg.

A hiker (below) trudges steadily along a mountain path in the wilds of Injasuti in the Drakensberg of KwaZulu-Natal.

*G*OLD RUSH

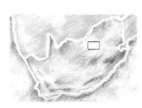

THE HIGHVELD was once a vast area of open grassland, or veld, dotted with occasional trees. The discovery of gold in the 1880s and its subsequent exploitation, however, has changed the face of the veld forever and nowhere is this more so than where, in an almost continuous wedge, urban development stretches from Pretoria in the north down to and along the Witwatersrand (which incorporates Johannesburg, South Africa's largest city, and its neighbour, Soweto) through to the towns of the East Rand – Benoni, Boksburg and Springs. The conurbation spreads on, down to Vereeniging on the Vaal River, to complete the financial and industrial heartland of Gauteng, where more than four million people live and find their work.

The veld beyond the urban sprawl has not escaped either, for the areas that are not given over to farmland and smaller country towns are dominated by the machinery of coal and gold mines and colossal power stations, petro-chemical plants and factories that belch their fumes into the atmosphere.

Here and there, the natural environment has a tenuous toe-hold; for example, the Magaliesberg range to the west of Pretoria, the Pilanesberg National Park adjacent to Sun City and a number of smaller but important areas of sanctuary.

Traditional dancing (left) is one of the principal recreations of mine-workers on the Reef, and tourists can enjoy the stirring rhythms of Africa at Gold Reef City on the outskirts of Johannesburg, where the city allows a glimpse of itself in its early years.

Upmarket shopping malls are synonymous with South African cities, but nowhere more so than in Johannesburg's northern suburbs. Sandton City (left) is one of the largest in the country where everything from supermarkets, department stores, cinemas, boutiques and other specialty shops as well as a five-star hotel are housed under one roof.

The contrasting faces of Johannesburg are strikingly obvious in the city's financial heart where the diamond-like edifice of '11 Diagonal Street' (right) looms over the few remaining buildings of a bygone era and the cluttered shops (below) that spill out their wares onto the pavement to entice the passers by.

The skyline of central Johannesburg (overleaf) stands out in the fading light of late evening.

Football, or soccer, as it is more widely known, has the greatest following of any spectator sport in South Africa. The country has always had its share of sportsmen of world class, but years of political isolation stunted their real potential, particularly in team events. This is changing rapidly with the return to the world arena. Clashes between South Africa and other countries, as well as top local sides, such as Kaiser Chiefs (yellow) and Hellenic (blue) shown above, fill the stadiums to capacity.

A rugby crowd at Johannesburg's Ellis Park (right). The game is passionately followed by many South Africans, starved of international competition for more than a decade since 1980, the year in which an official tour of the country was made by a British side. The new era that followed the end of apartheid saw the Rugby World Cup competition held in South Africa in 1995, with the winner's trophy going to the host country at Ellis Park in a nail-biting final against New Zealand.

Dolobran, a superb example of colonial architecture (above), stands proud atop Parktown Ridge. Homes such as these were built along the ridge of the 'Rand of Lords', the financial and industrial moguls of the Witwatersrand in its early years. But for the communications tower intruding on the skyline, a reminder of the city bustle south of the ridge, the wooded setting could be that of a grand country estate.

The name 'Soweto' is instantly recognized throughout the world. A huge, sprawling place, Soweto is home to some two million people. Although there are areas of obvious wealth and, at the other extreme, the makeshift shacks of a shanty town, most of the residents live in these endless rows of characterless 'match box' houses (right).

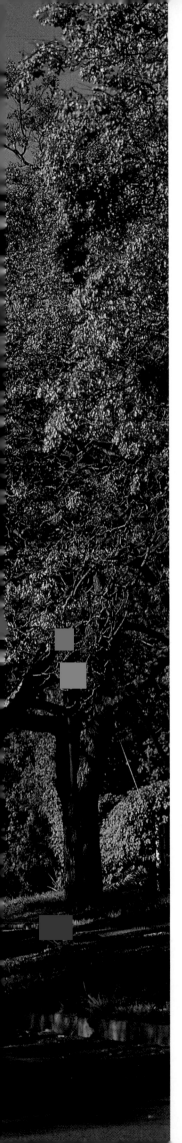

Purple blooms of jacaranda (left) brighten the summer streets of Pretoria. In its earliest years, however, Pretoria was known as a town of roses, but became the 'Jacaranda City' in 1888 when the first jacaranda trees – imported from Brazil at the then high price of ten pounds apiece – were planted. In the distance are the Union buildings on Pretoria's Meintjies Kop, the administrative headquarters of the South African government. They are the most ambitious of architect Sir Herbert Baker's South African work – he even specified what sorts of trees and shrubs should be planted in the sculpted amphitheatre.

A bearded old man in a Pretoria street festival (right), dressed in the style of the pioneers of a bygone time.

The razzle-dazzle of Sun City (left), where an unbelievable pleasure dome of hotels, casinos, theatres, cinemas and sports facilities of all descriptions has been created out of the surrounding scrubland. This ambitious and commercially highly successful venture draws the city dwellers of nearby Johannesburg and Pretoria in their droves, especially at weekends and holiday times. Aside from gambling and general good living, Sun City offers entertainment ranging from extravaganzas, boxing and wrestling title bouts, rock concerts and, the biggest drawcard of all, the Million Dollar golf tournament (bottom) every December. The dollars are 'US' and the players, among the world leaders, come by invitation only.

The Lost City (right), is the latest addition to this hedonistic Sun International creation, and boasts an impressive outdoor entertainment centre which has played host to the likes of Elton John and Jean-Michel Jarre. The Pilanesberg National Park lies just beyond the Lost City in an ancient volcanic crater.

The language of beads (above) expressed in this Ndebele apron, is complex, and understanding the significance of the patterns and colours requires considerable study. Beads were an important item of trade with African people since before the recorded period of southern African history. Some beads found at sites such as Mapungubwe in the Northern Province have been dated to the pre-Christian era.

The decorations on an Ndebele hut in the Northern Province (left) are traditionally the work of the women, whose personal adornments are also bright and colourful. Commerically obtainable paints have replaced natural pigments such as ochre, enabling a wider range of colours to be employed. Some of this woman's ornaments, such as the loops around her neck, arms and legs, cannot be removed.

41

TROUT STREAMS AND WATERFALLS

THE MPUMALANGA ESCARPMENT, where the mighty Drakensberg falls away almost sheer to the Lowveld, is an enchanting land of wood and water, mists and mountains. Here, memories of the prospector's lonely fire beneath the star-hung and limitless African sky are revived at the quiet 1870s village of Pilgrim's Rest, a name that somehow seems apt. But perhaps a thousand years before that, other prospectors, men of the African Iron Age, built forges here, and worked their metal.

Just as varied as the changing patterns of humanity, is the range of attractions of this northerly part of South Africa. Streams once panned for precious gold dust or diverted to wash mounds of crushed ore are today the haunt of trout, and the tree-lined banks shade contented anglers. Rivers flow slow and placid between shady banks, to crash suddenly over sheer cliffs, making rainbows dance in the fine flung spray.

Plantations of pines and eucalyptus dominate the landscape, but here and there mountains still shelter patches of primaeval forest that is home to chattering monkeys and shy antelope. The pilgrims still come, no longer seeking gold, but the peace and beauty that earlier visitors all too often overlooked.

From his float-ring (left), an angler casts a lazy line as the sun sets near Dullstroom. The cool, high land of the Mpumalanga Escarpment is a mecca for South African fly-fishermen and every weekend the lodges are filled with devotees seeking momentary relief from the tensions of city life.

Young Venda women (above) perform the python-dance to the steady rhythm of drums in the firelight. The dance is performed in the morning and evening and takes place at the end of the *domba*, an initiation period of several months, during which the girls are prepared for marriage and adult life.

At Lone Creek Falls (right) on a tributary of the Sabie River, the water plunges 68 metres into a cool, forested gorge. Close by are also the Bridal Veil and Sabie falls, all within a few kilometres of the forestry town of Sabie. After flowing through the Kruger National Park, the Sabie River joins the Komati River close to Mozambique.

Descending from the village of
Haenertsburg to Tzaneen,
Magoebaskloof (left) is a scenic delight
of forest and water. Here on the
northern edge of the escarpment,
sculpted terraces are densely planted
with tea which thrives in the moist
subtropical climate. This relatively
new, but flourishing industry is labour
intensive and provides employment for
local tea pickers (above). Increased
local production has reduced South
Africa's dependence on tea imports
from Sri Lanka.

The Blyde River Canyon (right) shrouded in early morning mist. From the Highveld the Blyde River falls more than 1 000 metres down the escarpment to the hot, humid bushveld. Over time the river has cut through the softer rocks to carve the only true canyon in South Africa and one of the great scenic wonders of the country. From the summit of the sheer quartzite cliffs, the river seems little more than a sparkling thread as it rushes down to the turbulent confluence of the Blyde and Treur rivers where large potholes (below) have been eroded by the swirling of suspended matter. In the 1870s a prospector named Bourke found gold here, and the place is still known as Bourke's Luck. The rivers were named by Voortrekkers who, fearing the worst when a scouting party failed to return, called the first *Treur*, meaning sorrow. Soon after, however, their mourning turned to joy as the party returned in safety, and they named the second *Blyde*, meaning glad.

Approaching Pilgrim's Rest (top), the road winds down as it did years ago when the stage coach was held up and robbed at gun-point. The hold-up was not a complete success, and on his release from prison, the former robber returned to the town and established the Highwayman's Garage. Pilgrim's Rest dates back to 1873, when a prospector, known as Wheelbarrow Alex because he transported all his belongings around in a barrow, struck gold in a nearby creek, and for a while the town grew and flourished. The heady days of 'gold rush' are long past, but the carefully preserved village retains much of its early character.

The general dealer's store (bottom) no longer does business, but visitors can contemplate the items that their grandmothers might have bought in years gone by. Although the village itself consists of simply constructed houses, the manager's house, a short distance away, is a complete contrast. This mansion now serves as a museum, tastefully filled with treasures from the Art Nouveau and Art Deco periods.

The road to Cybele Forest Lodge (right) is wreathed in a gentle mist of autumn, as fallen jacaranda flowers, still colourful, line its edges. Close to the little town of White River, the lodge is a favourite with people who, while getting away from it all, enjoy the fine cuisine of an establishment that is a member of the Paris-based Relais et Château chain.

BIG GAME COUNTRY

THE LOWVELD. For many people the term Lowveld, or Bushveld, conjures up images of the old-time professional hunter, and of the trader's wagon creaking across the vast stretch of Africa, scourged by malaria and bilharzia, between the escarpment and the sea at Delagoa Bay. The trader finally settled and opened his store, to flourish or fail as fortune decreed. Medical science has made enormous strides in conquering the diseases of man and his beasts that were invariably death-sentences in bygone days. And the hunter, having come close to exterminating the wild game, finally made way for the conservationist.

On the Lowveld is one of the world's most ambitious and successful attempts to conserve wildlife, the Kruger National Park. Here in an area of nearly 20 000 square kilometres (two-thirds the size of Belgium and as large as Wales) lion, rhino and elephant move safe in their majesty through countryside little changed in hundreds of thousands of years. On the grassy plains, acacias spread their umbrella-like crowns in contrast to those strange, stunted giants of nature, the baobabs. The richness and diversity of the Park is awe inspiring: at least 147 species of mammals occur, more than 450 species of trees and over 500 species of birds. Some 500 000 people visit the Kruger each year from all over the world, but their numbers as well as the camps and infrastructure to accommodate them are lost in the vastness of it all.

An adult lion (*Panthera leo*) (left), regal and unafraid, directs his yellow-eyed gaze straight at the camera.

The African elephant (*Loxodonta africana*) (left) is the largest of the land mammals. With its immense bulk and strength goes a gentleness towards others of its kind and a strong social sense. Elephants have no natural enemies other than man, but this has proved problem enough for the animals. In the last century they were hunted mercilessly and in 1912 only 25 remained in the Sabi Game Reserve which was to become the nucleus of the Kruger National Park. Today, although animals still fall prey to poachers for their ivory, the elephant population has grown towards the estimated maximum capacity of between 7 000 and 8 000.

A hippo (*Hippopotomus amphibius*) (above) 'yawns', displaying its impressive gape. Despite its ungainly, almost comical appearance on land, in water the hippo shows itself to be an adept and graceful swimmer. An interesting aspect of the animal is its lack of hair, the absence of sweat glands and its very thin epidermis over a thick dermis. This means that a hippo is heavily dependent on deep water, spending much of the day sub-merged to avoid dehydration which can result in the cracking of its skin.

The bushveld (previous page) under lowering clouds, is briefly coloured by the arc of a rainbow.

The white-fronted bee-eater (*Merops bullockoides*) (left) is a common resident species in the Lowveld, but is usually found near flowing rivers. Despite its name this species feeds mainly on butterflies, but bees and other insects also form part of its diet. Prey is caught on the wing, either by soaring or by darting from its perch.

Only the male impala (*Aepyceros melampus*) (right) has the characteristic lyre-shaped horns. Impala are the most numerous antelope species in the Lowveld and form a very important part of the diet of larger predators. They are highly gregarious and most frequently seen in herds of 10 to 50 animals.

A leaping impala (below) is frozen by the camera in a graceful, balletic stretch. At a single leap, impala can clear a height of three metres and cover a distance of up to 10 metres.

Safari in style (above) on one of the private reserves bordering the Kruger National Park. At these luxury lodges, guests can enjoy the comforts of five-star accommodation and cuisine. Open four-wheel-drive vehicles enable visitors to experience the thrill of close encounters with the 'big five', including the buffalo (*Syncerus caffer*) (left). This highly adaptable species is found widely throughout the Lowveld game reserves. Although they may seem placid while grazing or ruminating peacefully, buffalo are extremely temperamental and can be formidable fighters. If alarmed they often snort loudly and dash away to the bush but, if cows and calves are present, they might take up a defensive attitude with the bulls forming a protective ring around them.

Cape vultures (*Gyps coprotheres*) (below) gather on a giraffe kill temporarily abandoned by the rightful owners – probably a pride of lions. Although relatively safe in the protected area of the Mpumalanga reserves, the largest breeding colonies of Cape vultures occur farther afield in cattle-ranching country. Owing to the practice of ranchers burying dead beasts to prevent the spreading of disease, the vulture's food supply has been seriously diminished. The species is also threatened by the irresponsible practice by certain farmers of poisoning carcasses to eradicate jackals and scavenging dogs.

A giraffe (*Giraffa camelopardalis*) (right) shows the characteristic splay-legged stance necessary for the animal to reach the water. When drinking, with the raising and lowering of the head through the long arc of the neck, the giraffe's unique circulatory system regulates what would be sudden and fatal changes in blood pressure. In this awkward position, giraffes are particularly vulnerable to an attack by lion and it is common for them to drink in turn while others stand watch. The giraffe is the tallest living creature with bulls reaching heights of over five metres. Like most other mammals, the giraffe has only seven neck bones.

The tree squirrel (*Paraxerus cepapi*) (top) usually makes its home in a hollow tree, but actually spends most of its waking time on the ground, foraging for small insects, roots and grasses.

Hikers, guided by game rangers (above), make their way along a path on the Bushman Wilderness Trail in the Kruger National Park. Trails are operated regularly throughout the year in most areas of the Park as well as other nearby reserves, providing a rare opportunity for game-viewing on foot.

A young leopard (*Panthera pardus*) (right), silent and secretive, goes about its business in the dark. Leopards are shy, solitary creatures and hunt mainly at night, their prey being anything from insects, fish, birds and reptiles to mammals up to the size of a kudu. Impala, however, make up the major part of the leopard's diet.

The long-striding cheetah (*Acinonyx jubatus*) (overleaf) is the fastest of all land mammals and can reach a speed of almost 100 kilometres per hour.

A wild dog (*Lycaon pictus*) (above), also known as the Cape Hunting Dog, is a fast and ferocious hunter. Moving in packs, wild dogs pursue their prey relentlessly, tearing chunks of flesh from the victim's body until it collapses. Then, instead of the animals rushing in to squabble over the carcass and with the stronger, more dominant animals taking the choicest bits, the adult dogs stand aside to allow the younger animals to feed first.

A chacma baboon (*Papio ursinus*) (right), a parody of man, contemplates life by the roadside. Baboons usually move about in troops of up to 100 animals, in the charge of several dominant males. Their chief enemy is the leopard, but several large baboons, backed by the rest of the pack, may sometimes present a front so threatening that the leopard will back off.

A perching bateleur (*Terathopius ecaudatus*) (above) has a name said to derive from the French word for an acrobat, because of its supreme aerial skills and habit of tipping its wings in flight. It is easily distinguished from other birds of prey by its red legs and very short tail, beyond which its feet project when in flight.

An elephant feeds on at the red hour of sunset (right). These huge mammals spend most of their time eating and drinking to maintain their colossal bulk, and their consumption is impressive – individual animals may eat 150 to 300 kilograms of vegetation a day and, if they have access to water, drink as much as 180 to 220 litres a day.

HIGHLAND SPLENDOUR

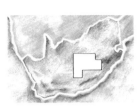

THE EASTERN FREE STATE AND THE KWAZULU-NATAL DRAKENSBERG. Between the coastal plain of KwaZulu-Natal and the Highveld of South Africa's central plateau are the great peaks of the Drakensberg, known to the indigenous people of the area as *Quathlamba*, the 'barrier of spears'. To the Voortrekkers the jagged peaks suggested the back of a dragon and they named the range the 'Drakensberge'. In those early days, the mountains formed an almost impenetrable barrier to travellers and even today only a few tortuous mountain passes provide routes up and through the precipitous escarpment. The Drakensberg's inaccessibility has ensured a sense of peace and tranquility, and here, in a string of wilderness areas, mountain peaks and reserves, is much to enjoy for the climber, the hiker, the wildlife enthusiast, and for those simply content to rest and savour some of the grandest scenery in South Africa.

Behind the Drakensberg are the wild and even more remote Maluti mountains in the kingdom of Lesotho. On the northeastern fringes of this mighty range, where Lesotho and the eastern Free State meet, is a landscape of natural sculptures carved by the wind from the Clarens Sandstone formed at the end of the age of the dinosaurs. In the low, slanting light of early morning and evening the huge and fantastic formations glow golden, shot with tinges of purple and brown, forming a spectacular back-drop for the Golden Gate Highlands National Park.

Poplars near Clarens in the eastern Free State (left), their rich autumnal foliage in a display which rivals the burnt hues of the surrounding sandstone buttresses.

The flowers of cosmos (above) are colourfully sprinkled throughout the fields and along the roadsides in KwaZulu-Natal and the Highveld. An annual herb of the family Compositae (sometimes known as Asteraceae), which is the largest family of flowering plants in the world, cosmos is a native of Central America.

A layered cliff of Clarens Sandstone (left) in the Golden Gate Highlands National Park forms a backdrop for a herd of peacefully grazing horses. Formerly the Cave Sandstone, it was so-named for the numerous caves and recesses that have been eroded over time at the base of the majestic cliffs. These natural shelters have through history given refuge to man, and as recently as two centuries ago, Bushman artists were still painting on the rocky walls.

The rare bearded vulture (*Gypaetus barbatus*) (left) more closely resembles an eagle in appearance, but has the vulture's scavenging habits of feeding primarily off bones and carrion. Once more widely distributed, it is now found only along the Drakensberg and the highlands of Lesotho and the eastern Free State. The bearded vulture, or lammergeier as it is sometimes known, has developed a unique method of dealing with the larger bones – it drops them from a great height onto a smooth slab of rock, repeating the process until the fragments are small enough to swallow.

In the Royal Natal National Park (right) hikers make their way down a rocky defile leading to panoramic views of the Drakensberg. As in Golden Gate, a favourite way of exploring this vast and scenic park is by horseback, while for hikers more than 30 trails have been marked out. Trout-fishing is another popular pastime. The park acquired its 'Royal' title after a visit by the British royal family in 1947.

The jackal buzzard (*Buteo rufofuscus*) (top) is a common resident of the mountains, and visitors to the Drakensberg are unlikely to miss seeing this masterful flier characteristically hanging as it rides the turbulence along cliff edges, studying the landscape for potential prey.

Bushman paintings (above) often depict eland, animals which held a special place in the lore of these people who have long vanished from the mountains. Eland were an important source of food, and their hides were probably used as coverings. Although many Bushman paintings are complex and very difficult to interpret, this one appears to show a hunting scene.

As winter comes to the Drakensberg (right) the shining green of the foothills or 'Little 'Berg' gives way to shades of yellow and brown. Winters in the KwaZulu-Natal uplands can often be bitterly cold and lasting snowfalls are common.

Devil's Tooth (previous page), a well-known and well-respected peak in the Drakensberg, overlooks the gorge of the Tugela River. This pinnacle defeated many attempts to scale its sheer sides and it was only in 1950 that it was conquered for the first time.

Cathkin Peak (above), seen through a break in the swirling clouds, reaches a height of 3 182 metres, and its summit was the target of two ambitious climbers many years ago. Confident of success, they took a bottle of champagne to celebrate their anticipated conquest, but failed to reach the top. The name of Champagne Castle was later applied to another peak, about three kilometres east of Cathkin.

The Tugela Falls cascade down a rugged Drakensberg cliff (right). In all there are five falls with a total drop of 853 metres, the longest single fall being 411 metres. This makes them the highest in southern Africa and, it is believed, the second highest in the world. The river's name comes from a Zulu word meaning 'one that startles', as the river certainly does when it is in raging flood.

Over the rolling farmlands of the KwaZulu-Natal hinterland, a microlight aircraft (above) provides its pilot with an eagle's-eye view.

A mansion in a forest clearing in the KwaZulu-Natal Midlands (left) provides a local version of one of the stately homes of England. Although it was briefly a Boer republic, the province has a strong British heritage and is often facetiously referred to as 'the last outpost of the Empire'. Under a treaty with Shaka, the Zulu king, a few Englishmen formed a trading settlement on the shores of Durban Bay as long ago as the 1820s. Some 4 000 English settlers arrived around 1850, and a town such as Pietermaritzburg, despite its name, has a distinct Englishness in its late Victorian architecture.

In Loteni Nature Reserve (previous page), a quiet road winds into the hills. This remote sanctuary nestling beneath the high crags of the majestic Drakensberg is a trout-fisherman's paradise.

ZULU KINGDOM

WILDLIFE HERITAGE AND TRADITIONAL HOME OF THE ZULU PEOPLE, whose name means 'sky' or 'heaven', the old Zulu kingdom has some of the finest inland and marine nature reserves in southern Africa. Some preserve romantic names from the past, but none are more magical than those given by the Zulu: *Dlinza* or *Hlinza* means 'place of tomb-like meditation', *Sodwana* means 'little one on its own' while *Bonamanzi* tells of 'good water'.

Maputaland is the far northern part of KwaZulu-Natal leading to the Mozambique border. This is a vast wilderness area, some 9 000 square kilometres in extent, of wonderful beauty and diversity. Here, in a few reserves visitors may elect to sleep in tree-houses, some of which even have the dining and sitting rooms up in the branches. Anglers can delight in one of the largest lakes in South Africa, said to hold the greatest variety of freshwater fish, and sea fishermen cluster the beaches and steer their powerboats out through gaps in the reefs.

Conservationists warn that this subtropical paradise is environmentally extremely fragile, and have defined no fewer than 21 different but often interdependent ecosystems, including beaches, swamps, flood-plains and forests. Sadly, the region is also one of great poverty, but at the same time as addressing the plight of local people, the preservation of the natural environment is one of the most urgent imperatives facing conservationists.

Burchell's zebra (*Equus burchellii*) (left) is unmistakably a member of the horse family and is widely found throughout the plains of sub-Saharan Africa.

The Itala Game Reserve is one of KwaZulu-Natal's showpieces. The attractive Ntshondwe Camp (above), overlooking a waterhole, offers superb game-viewing.

The white rhino (*Ceratotherium simum*) (left), is second in size only to the elephant. At the turn of the present century, the white (or square-lipped) rhino had been hunted almost to the point of extinction and the only remaining population was that protected in the Umfolozi section of the Hluhluwe-Umfolozi Park. Under the dedicated management of a handful of Parks Board personnel, the animals flourished and today white rhinos are regularly 'exported' to be reintroduced widely throughout their former range.

Only the male black-bellied korhaan (*Eupodotis melanogaster*) (right) has a black belly, the female having a white front. These birds are usually seen in pairs, often close to marshy ground where the grass is not too long to conceal the approach of an enemy.

The cry of the fish eagle (*Haliaeetus vocifer*) is one of the most stirring sounds of untamed Africa, a loud, yelping echo uttered even when soaring. Its days are spent atop tall trees, watching the surface of a lake or river for some telltale sign of a fish moving near the surface. Then, in a smooth glide, the fish eagle closes in and snatches the fish, scarcely pausing in its flight. Deeper swimming fish are not altogether safe from the talons of this powerful raptor as it is know to submerge completely in its determination to reach its prey.

A lioness and a thorn tree (right) catch the low-slanting light in the area of the Hluhluwe-Umfolozi Park. These are probably the two best-known reserves in KwaZulu-Natal, and the corridor that unites them is some eight kilometres wide, adding a further 21 000 hectares to the conservation area.

Sodwana Bay National Park
(opposite), where the fresh waters of
Lake Mgobeseleni reach the sea in the
shelter of Jesser Point, is a haven for
anglers. It is fortunate to have been
preserved as a nature area, as it was
seriously considered for a harbour
development. The site eventually chosen
was 120 kilometres to the south, at
Richards Bay, and so anglers and divers
still drive the long road to Sodwana in
happy anticipation of their sport.

The rare leatherback turtle
(*Dermochelys coriacea*) (left, above)
lays her eggs on a sandy beach north of
Sodwana Bay, after laboriously digging
a hole with her front flippers. After
laying as many as 120 eggs, she
carefully covers them with sand before
starting her slow trek back to the sea.
Hatchlings emerge after about 70 days
under cover of darkness to escape
heavy predation by crabs and gulls.

A xanthid crab (left, centre) moves
ponderously across the sand at Cape
Vidal on the eastern shores of St Lucia.
These cumbersome crabs have
characteristically large nippers which
are used to good effect in crushing the
shells of their prey.

A pretty clownfish (*Amphiprion* spp.)
(left, below). This small, colourful fish
is widespread in tropical waters and is
always found sheltering in sea
anemones. This complex symbiotic
relationship ensures that the fish is at
least partially immune to the stinging
tentacles. The anemone apparently
'recognizes' its resident clownfish and
refrains from stinging it whereas it will
attack imposters.

A young bushbuck ram (*Tragelaphus scriptus*) (right) stares anxiously for a split second before fleeing into the waterside undergrowth at False Bay, which is the northernmost of the St Lucia reserves, and which has the only breeding colony of pink-backed pelicans in South Africa. Bushbuck tend to be solitary and rest up during the heat of the day, emerging only in the late afternoon to feed into the night.

The malachite kingfisher (*Alcedo cristata*) (left), despite its bright colouring, may be difficult to see when it is sitting motionless on a shady branch. It dives at great speed from its perch to capture its food consisting of small fish, tadpoles and flying insects. The malachite kingfisher nests in tunnels excavated in river banks, using its long, pointed bill to dig its burrow.

A painted reed frog (*Hyperolius marmoratus*) (left, below), which grows to a length of only three centimetres, peers cautiously between the leaves. These frogs gather in large numbers around permanent water and when a few hundred call in unison, the noise is almost deafening.

Anglers at St Lucia (above) exchange tales as lines tighten over the darkening water. Angling is by far South Africa's greatest participator sport and is especially popular here as the waters team with fish.

Hippopotamus at St Lucia (left) show just the tops of their heads while enjoying a wallow in the shallow waters at sunset. When darkness has fallen they will wander ashore in search of food, each animal consuming up to 180 kilograms of vegetation nightly.

AFRICAN RAJ

DURBAN, PIETERMARITZBURG AND THE COASTAL PLAYGROUND. Echoes of empire linger in odd corners of old Natal (now known as KwaZulu-Natal).

The heritage of the province is far more than just British, however. Settlers from India, and their descendants, are most numerous around Durban and Pietermaritzburg, where their distinctive dress, not completely lost to western attire, and architecture lend a touch of the East to this southern land. Dutch-descended Voortrekkers made their mark too, and the oldest house in Pietermaritzburg, the joint provincial capital (together with Ulundi), was built by one of these pioneers. But above all else, KwaZulu-Natal is the home of the Zulu-speaking people, who number more than six million, making them the largest language group in the entire country.

Durban is primarily 'holiday city', but at the same time is South Africa's busiest harbour and has a substantial industrial sector. It lies around a bay, protected from the open sea by two promontories, the Point in the north, and the sandy, bush-covered Bluff in the south. The coastal plain which contains the central city extends inland for only a kilometre or two before rising steeply towards the Berea, one of Durban's more affluent suburbs, and the seemingly endless rolling hills that reach out to the mighty Drakensberg.

Tall masts in Durban's yacht basin (left) are dwarfed by the high-rise buildings of the city centre in the background. The tower blocks of the city centre are close to the site where Shaka allowed the first white settlers to build their hut of wattle and daub back in 1824.

Durban's Golden Mile (left), the long, continuous stretch of hotels that line the city's beachfront. Here the quiet dignity of 'The Edward', redolent of colonial times, is interrupted by a concrete and glass forest of more glitzy establishments such as the Elangeni, the Maharani, complete with turbaned doorman, and many others. In the foreground is the beachfront funfair with its overhead cableway.

A boardsailor becomes airborne (above) off a Durban beach. Experienced boardsailors are to be seen in action off the beach opposite the Snake Park at most times of the year, although locals say that the month of May provides the best conditions.

A bottle-nosed dolphin (*Tursiops truncatus*) (above right) at Sea World, one of the main attractions of the beachfront where visitors and locals alike are drawn to the aquarium and dolphinarium complex. Sea World is also an important institute for marine biological research.

SOUTH TO EDEN

THE WILD COAST, EASTERN CAPE AND THE GARDEN ROUTE. Long beaches and rocky headlands are very much the physical character of South Africa's eastern seaboard, but especially so along the remote Wild Coast of the Eastern Cape. Here the undulating hills and valleys that march coastwards from the western limits of the Drakensberg often end abruptly in sheer cliffs and rocky headlands. Herein lies the 'wildness' where the dramatic interaction of sea and shore have created magnificent features such as Hole-in-the-Wall, and Waterfall Bluff, where the river plunges clear into the turbulent surf. Vast rocky reefs extend far out to sea. A fisherman's paradise, the Wild Coast was, and still is, a mariner's nightmare; many a ship from the mid-16th century right up to the present has foundered here.

The roads to the coves and villages by the sea are rough and tortuous, for the main highway threads its way inland past hillsides dotted with rural settlements, returning to the sea at East London before making a loop that includes the 'Settler City' of Grahamstown. Another road runs directly between East London and Port Elizabeth, following the coast more closely, passing lovely river estuaries and lagoons, and the former harbour of Port Alfred. A short way to the west begins one of the most beautiful parts of a beautiful land, a region that, for its sheer magnificence of mountain, forest and water, has been named the Garden Route.

A typical view along the coast (left) where the sheer visual beauty of the landscape often masks the great poverty of the rural communities that dot the hillside.

A young lad in a rural area (right).
It is often the charge of young boys to
tend their fathers' cattle and along the
country roads it is a common sight
to come across large herds being
marshalled by a few youngsters
dwarfed by the beasts around them.

A Xhosa-speaking woman (left)
carries live chickens atop her elaborate
turban which shows her to be a matron
of standing in her community. Through
acculturation the strictly traditional
forms of dress have largely disappeared,
giving way to more western styles. In the
remoter parts, however, the garments
and ornaments of yesteryear are still
worn but probably only ceremonially.

A new highway and modern bridges
such as this one (above) carry the
traveller effortlessly through the
Tsitsikamma Forest. First of the
'modern' bridges was that over the
Storms River, built in 1956, arching
some 137 metres above the river. The
old passes wound through steep gorges
into the heart of the forest.

Natural forest clings to the crags (left)
along the deeply eroded gorge of the
Bobbejaans (baboons) River in the
Garden Route's Tsitsikamma Forest.

The glorious Tsitsikamma coastline
(right) falls within a national park
that conserves areas of both forest and
of sea. Many walking trails invite the
more energetic visitors to enjoy the
natural wonders of this part of the
Garden Route at close range.

The modern holiday complex on Beacon Isle (above) at Plettenberg Bay occupies the site of an old Norwegian whaling station, and a few of the large iron blubber-pots are still to be seen. The little island, at the mouth of the Piesang (banana) River, was named for the wooden navigational beacon erected there in 1772. The Piesang River, in turn, was named for the wild bananas (*Strelitzia alba*) that grew along its pleasant, grassy banks.

The wide beaches of Plettenberg Bay (right), as well as lagoons and the forested hinterland, make the area a popular rendezvous for holiday-makers. Early Portuguese explorers named it *Babia Formosa* — 'beautiful bay' — while the indigenous peoples knew the area as Tsitsikamma, or 'shining waters'; a reference perhaps both to the sea and to the many sparkling rivers that flow through the region.

Knysna Lagoon (overleaf) is enclosed by forested banks leadings to a narrow sea entrance between two impressive sandstone bluffs known as 'The Heads'.

The Outeniqua choo-Tjoe (left), pulled by a class 24 steam locomotive, follows one of the world's most scenic rail routes from George to Knysna through field and forest and lakelands. Over part of its journey, the train hugs the rugged coastline, affording breath-taking vistas of sea and mountain.

Many craftsmen and hobbyists have turned their pastimes to profit to enable themselves to live, many of them very simply indeed, in the beautiful Knysna district. Items of leatherwork, and handcrafts, furniture and utensils of local timber, are displayed for sale within the premises of this 19th century house (left).

Millwood House (right) in Knysna was once erected as part of the gold rush town of Millwood in the nearby forest. Today it is a museum of local history while the peace of the forests has reclaimed the old gold-workings. A few signposts, fruit trees and garden flowers are almost the only reminders of the fleeting days of glory.

ACROSS THE PLAINS OF CAMDEBOO

THE LONELY HILLS AND FLATS OF THE KAROO seem to the hot, weary traveller to stretch endlessly ahead and this vast hinterland is often facetiously referred to as 'miles and miles of bloody Africa'. But for anyone who pauses to explore the byways and small towns or 'dorps', the Karoo has a charm which repays the effort. For this is the quintessential 'platteland' of South Africa — the rural heartland of windmills, sheep-runs and the hospitable hearth, of dolerite-capped hills, or 'koppies', and of corrugated iron sheet that has been bent and beaten to serve almost any function. Camdeboo is just one corner of this great semi-arid region, the name of which derives from a Khoisan word thought to mean 'green hollow', a seeming misnomer for although the Karoo can show a gentle face of lush veld and flora, this only happens after the rains, and for the greater part of the year the landscape is dusty and dry. But the Karoo — moody and mysterious — is worth far more than just the cursory glance that most travellers give it. Here, Kipling's 'wonderful north-bound train' sweeps past a complete, preserved Victorian village and continues its way under the silent gaze of blockhouses built almost a century ago to guard the line at vulnerable points. Villages dot the land, most of them as far from the next as one day's journey by ox-wagon, and each proud of its Dutch Reformed church building that, to the stranger, seems too large for its setting.

A donkey cart (left) and passengers make their way slowly but steadily across the timeless Karoo landscape.

Horses and ostriches (left) feed in a field near Calitzdorp in the Little Karoo, close to the Swartberg or 'black mountains'. Ungainly though it may seem, the ostrich (*Struthio camelus*) is extremely swift, and can easily outrun a man. For a flightless bird this speed is its only escape from danger, but it will also stand its ground and attack viciously when courting, or when guarding its nest, and the kick of an ostrich – it kicks forward and downward with its spur-clawed feet – has been known to disembowel a man at one stroke. A local delicacy of the region is the ostrich egg omelette, full of flavour but very rich. Each egg is equivalent to about 24 ordinary hen's eggs.

Elaborate 'feather palaces' such as the one shown here (above) sprouted about the countryside of the Little Karoo as the demand for ostrich feathers soared in the days before the First World War when the plumes, especially those of the male bird, were an essential accessory in the *haute couture* of the time. Although the fashion changed and the industry built around it died, a few 'show farms' survive on the passing tourist trade and the far more modest commercial use of ostrich feathers.

The Valley of Desolation (overleaf), a forbiddingly barren area of the Karoo, viewed from a high ridge where basaltic pillars rise as high as 120 metres.

Strydenburg is a typical Karoo 'dorp' or small town (left). Time seems to stand still in such small towns where the general store is a focus of the community and, contrary to current thinking elsewhere, advertisements championing the consumption of tobacco are prominently displayed.

Graaff-Reinet's Dutch Reformed Church (right) is the third to be built on the same commanding site. Described by one authority as 'hideously magnificent', the church was begun in 1886 and incorporates many mass-produced decorations in stone and iron. To the non-critical observer, however, it is an impressive pile, particularly the tower, of which about half the height consists of the spire. The church houses a fine collection of old Cape silver.

A house in Richmond (right) is richly decorated with lacy cast iron. Fashionable in Victorian times and after, most of the cast iron that mushroomed throughout South Africa, from simple rails to complete and complex memorials, came from the Saracen Foundry of Walter MacFarlane in Glasgow. Much of it was torn down and destroyed with development and the passing of fashion, but its charm has been 'rediscovered' with a resurgence of nostalgia for the art and ephemera of Victorian times, especially in the cities.

The long and lonely road (overleaf) runs through the golden Karoo, a vast region of low rainfall and extreme temperatures. Its plant cover is sparse, but unique in the way it has adapted to survive the harsh conditions. These prickly pears are not indigenous.

THE FLOWERING DESERT

THIRSTLANDS OF THE BARREN NORTH AND WEST. The Karoo extends far to the north and west, where true desert conditions are encountered in the Namib of Namibia and the Kalahari of the far Northern Cape and Botswana. But the baking plains of sand and rock are not without life, from tiny lizards to the king of beasts himself. Rain is scarce, but when the winter falls have been relatively good, especially in that section close to the coast and known as Namaqualand, the display of spring flowers is staggering. A visitor needs to see the countryside in its barren state, as well as in flower, in order to fully appreciate the magical transformation.

Scattered with diamonds here and there, the area, for most of its occupants, is nevertheless a poor one and life is hard. Communally owned farming reserves are found dotted about Namaqualand, their location dictated by a source of permanent water. One of these, Leliefontein, was granted as long ago as 1771. For many people though, there is no such security, and they must move from town to remote town, from farm to farm, in an often vain search for work. Gypsy-like, they are seen along lonely roads and busy highways, on creaking carts pulled by patient donkeys or, more often, walking, endlessly it seems, with a small bundle of possessions, to some unknown destination.

The roar of water at Augrabies (left) is deafening where the mighty Orange River, the border between South Africa and Namibia, forces itself through a narrow gap in the granite rock, to plunge deep into the gorge it has scoured with the passing of time. The cataract is the central feature of the surrounding Augrabies Falls National Park.

The Cape eagle owl (*Bubo capensis*) (opposite), widespread but thinly distributed, may sometimes be seen during the day, resting up in the branches of a tall tree or, in the early morning or late afternoon, sunning itself on a rock. At dusk it moves to hunt from some favourite perch lower down, uttering its characteristic, hooting call. Its prey comprises mainly hares and hyraxes (dassies) and these are often hunted from roadside vantage points such as telegraph poles and fence posts. A sad consequence of this is that many owls are killed by passing vehicles.

The secretarybird (*Sagittarius serpentarius*) (left) is an accomplished snake killer, despatching them in a blur of rapid kicks.

Perhaps through sheer joy of life, springbok (*Antidorcas marsupialis*) (below) make these sudden high leaps as though clearing imaginary obstacles, but no doubt a herd scattering and leaping does help to confuse predators. Another antic which comes into play when the animals are under stress or being chased is 'stotting' which consists of a stiff-legged vertical leap with back arched and a tuft of white hair along the ridge of the back expanded. Springbok are gregarious and move about in small herds, but larger groups are not uncommon and herds of thousands strong may come together to migrate in search of food and water. Gone though are the days when immense congregations of migratory springbok took days to pass by.

The ears of the bat-eared fox (*Otocyon megalotis*) (left above) are remarkably sensitive and play an important part in locating the animal's diet of insects. Walking slowly with head held low and ears outspread, it can clearly hear the sounds of insects burrowing underground and, having pinpointed the exact site, commences to dig for its dinner.

The yellow mongoose (*Cynictis penicillata*) (left centre) is not as gregarious as some of the other members of the mongoose family, and usually occurs in small family groups. Burrows are often shared with other species such as the ground squirrel (*Xerus inauris*) and suricate (*Suricata suricatta*). The yellow mongoose spends a great deal of time digging, either enlarging and adapting its underground home or in its quest for food which, apart from insects, also includes tiny mammals.

The black-backed jackal (*Canis mesomelas*) (left below), a cheeky opportunist, is an efficient hunter of mammals up to the size of hares and will also take insects, reptiles and birds. But is it also a scavenger and is quick to take advantage of the kills of larger predators. Jackal packs will discreetly trail lions or other big cats during the hunt and then pace impatiently up and down waiting for their turn at the meal.

A courting pair of lions (right) in the Kalahari Gemsbok National Park. Lions are fairly sociable animals, and are usually found in family groups of up to six animals, or in prides of up to 20. Chauvinists to the end, males allow the females to do most of the work of the hunt, but insist on being first to feed.

An inhabitant of the dry plains, the gemsbok (*Oryx gazella*) (previous page) is skilled at finding sources of moisture, most often from wild melons or by unearthing succulent roots. It is thus able to survive almost indefinitely without drinking – an obvious advantage in this dry land where water is scarce.

140

The lighthouse at Cape Columbine (right) lies in the Columbine Nature Reserve, where some of the rich flora of the Sandveld is preserved. Most of the flowers are at their showiest in spring, but the spectacular candelabra flower (*Brunsvigia orientalis*) usually displays its bright red, radiating flower heads in late summer.

A Doringbaai fisherman (right below) stands at the door of his cottage that has weathered the storms of decades. There is a fish-canning factory at Doringbaai, and fishing boats (left) also bring in more lucrative harvests of rock lobsters, as well as offshore diamonds. Just a few kilometres to the north is the long beach of Strandfontein, which is the seaside resort for the Sandveld, as this part of the Western Cape is known.

When spring comes to the West Coast (previous page) and inland Namaqualand, the veld is transformed into a tufted weave of flowers, especially after good winter rains. Here at St Helena Bay a fisherman's white-washed home is, for a few short weeks, in the midst of a radiant natural garden.

*T*HE FAIREST CAPE

THE CAPE PENINSULA AND THE WINELANDS at the southwestern tip of Africa enjoy a mild Mediterranean climate, and scenery and flora that are unsurpassed. Ringed by stately mountains, 'the Cape' is where settlers from Europe first landed in the southern part of Africa, and so, rare in the country, is able to number among its attractions interesting old buildings, a few dating back to the late 17th century. Although Cape Town, and its environs, is among the fastest growing cities in the world, the pace of life is more measured, less frenetic, than that of the stock exchange driven Witwatersrand to the north. Its supposedly lackadaisical business practice is generally regarded with amused contempt by the more materialistic city-dwellers of Johannesburg; some indeed, refer to it almost derisively as 'the colony'. And yet, if the financial reward is reasonable, a transfer to the Cape is usually eagerly accepted. There must be something about it.

There are, for instance, its beaches, each with a distinctive atmosphere of its own, and most of them within easy reach of the city centre. There are its mountains, for admiring or for climbing, or for gentle strolls on grassy slopes. A short way inland is farming country, with golden wheatfields, fragrant fruit orchards and, best known of all, the rows of vines on farms where, for centuries, wine has been produced and a jealously held aspect of South African culture has evolved.

Table Bay (left) with the majestic Table Mountain as its backdrop, remains one of the most famous landfalls in the world. The sailing tradition lives on and the brightly coloured spinnakers of ocean-going yachts are a familiar sight during the weekend when sleek racers and broad-beamed cruisers ply the waters of the bay.

At Cape Town's old harbour (left) restaurants, pubs and hotels, shops and a maritime museum are today very much part of the 'scene' but for many years the city and its docklands were sadly separated. The Victoria and Alfred Waterfront development is a recent and ongoing project to re-unite Cape Town with the sea. The Alfred Basin was the city's first sheltered harbour, begun in 1860 when Queen Victoria's second son, Prince Alfred, tipped the first load of stones to commence the breakwater.

A Capetonian plays a cool saxophone (above left) during a summertime street festival. Music and a keen sense of rhythm come naturally to a great many of Cape Town's people, and is never far away, be it a classical concert, driving rock, marimba or soulful street jazz. There is always live entertainment to be found at the Victoria and Alfred Waterfront or at the nightclubs in the city centre. Some is informal, like the impromptu performance of this mime artist (above).

A steep, cobbled street in Bo-Kaap (left) leads down to the city centre, past small houses with attractive Georgian facades. This is upper Longmarket Street, where the Masjied Boorhaanol Mosque dates back to the 1880s, although the minaret is a fairly recent replacement. There are no fewer than nine mosques within the close confines of Bo-Kaap.

A young girl of the Bo-Kaap (right), one of the oldest residential areas of Cape Town, blends the features of Africa and the East. Most of the people of Bo-Kaap are descended from slaves, free men and political exiles sent to the Cape in the time of the Dutch East India Company, from about 1668 to 1790.

At Salt River market (overleaf), small dealers and housewives stock up on fruit and vegetables. Many of the vegetables sold here are grown close by, on the small market farms of the Cape Flats. The immense pressure of a rapidly expanding population is seeing traditional farmland disappear, usually under a welter of informal settlements or squatter camps.

Clifton is to South Africa (left, above, and right) what Copacabana is to Rio, or Monte Carlo and St Tropez are to continental Europe. Here, against a stunning backdrop of mountain dropping almost sheer to the sea and where houses, apartment blocks and hotels cling precariously to the steep slopes, are the bright, white sands of Clifton's crescent beaches. When summer comes, the sun-worshippers flock to the beaches to stake their claim to a towel-sized patch of sand. Luxury yachts and motor cruisers anchor just beyond the surf line. Clifton is a place to be seen, but seldom to swim — only a few brave the sea for even in mid-summer the waters tend to be icy.

Cape Point, with its guardian lighthouse, lies close to the southern tip of the Cape Peninsula. Below the towering cliffs and accessible only at low tide, is lonely Dias Beach (above), on which the remains of a floating crane lie rusting into oblivion. The most southerly tip of the Peninsula is the Cape of Good Hope, which forms the western buttress to Dias Beach.

Chapman's Peak Drive (left), one of the world's most scenic marine drives, is sculpted from the mountainside at the point where the sandstone overburden joins the basal granite. When driven from south to north there are breathtaking views of Hout Bay harbour snugly set in its curl of mountain. All along its route, there are vantage points where tourists may stop to admire the spectacular cliffs and seascape, but these viewsites are also the haunt of baboons. Unafraid of man, the baboons can be aggressive and tourists are warned not to feed them.

155

The mountain above Kalk Bay, on the wide sweep of False Bay, glows in the light of a drizzly dawn. 'Kalk' – commonly pronounced by English-speakers as 'cork' – comes from Dutch, and refers to the lime kilns that were established here centuries ago. Kalk Bay is noted today for its picturesque fishing harbour, with boats crewed by the descendants of Filipino settlers who arrived in the 1870s. For the adventurous, the mountains here are riddled with extensive caves.

A surfer works 'The Hoek' at Noordhoek during a southeasterly blow. Many spots along the coastline are world-renowned for their ideal surfing conditions, and numerous competitions, both local and international, are held here. Noordhoek's Long Beach is safer for surfing than for swimming, but it also provides space for long, leisurely walks on its clean white sands. The remains of the steamship *Kakapo* lie on the beach.

A Kramat, or Muslim shrine (right above), has been built at Klein Constantia, above the burial place of an Islamic scholar of long ago. Kramats at Robben Island, Signal Hill and Oudekraal form the Holy Circle around Cape Town, within which believers are safe from fire, famine, plague, earthquake and tidal wave.

The stately mansion of Groot Constantia (right below) is a classic of the Cape Dutch architectural style. Established as a wine estate in the late 17th century, Groot Constantia still produces excellent wines, and the mansion and old cellars are a museum reflecting a time of great elegance for the privileged rulers of the early Cape.

The dovecot on the farm Buitenverwachting ('beyond expectation') (left above) probably served as slave quarters. Relatively few of these outbuildings survive on old farms at the Cape, and some that do were designed to hold poultry or small livestock, while pigeons or doves, kept for the pot or for decorative purposes, occupied the loft. Together with Groot Constantia, Klein Constantia, Constantia Uitsig and Steenberg, Buitenverwachting forms the Constantia Wine Route where visitors can taste and buy the fine produce of the vine. The estate also has one of the finest restaurants in the Cape Peninsula.

The avenue of camphor trees at Kirstenbosch (left below) was planted in the 1890s, when the estate was owned by Cecil John Rhodes. Bequeathed to the nation with Rhodes's other properties, Kirstenbosch is now a botanical garden of international repute and is the headquarters of the National Botanical Gardens of South Africa. Despite the hundreds of thousands of visitors who throng through its gates each year, the gardens retain their air of serenity in the shelter of Table Mountain's towering eastern buttresses.

The hills and fields of Vergelegen
(above) (which means 'remotely
situated'), and the glorious oak avenue
(right), are part of an estate that once
belonged to an old Cape governor.
Wilhem Adriaan van der Stel succeeded
his father – the creator of Groot
Constantia – in 1699 and, soon after,
began developing a farm and mansion
in what was then the outlying district
known as Hottentots Holland. The
resentment of the ordinary burghers led
to accusations of maladministration,
and the younger Van der Stel was
recalled to Holland. His lands at the
Cape were divided, and his beautiful
house ordered to be demolished. This
instruction was obeyed only half-
heartedly and much of the splendour
of the gracious Cape Dutch homestead
at Vergelegen has been restored.

The homestead of Ida's Valley near Stellenbosch (above and right) dates from about 1790, although to this day nobody is certain of the identity of Ida. Whatever its origin, the name is associated in South Africa with one of the gems of Cape Dutch architecture, with ornate gables considered to be among the finest of their kind. The land was granted in 1683 to François Villon, one of the earliest French settlers at the Cape, and he built the present jonkershuis – traditionally the home of the eldest son. Villon's numerous South African descendants have long spelt their surname as Viljoen, a sort of metamorphosis that many names have undergone in this country.

Vines in soldierly ranks (previous page) surround a homestead in the Hex River Valley. This beautiful basin in the Cape Fold Mountains is the northern limit of grape growing in this corner of the Western Cape and is a region that exports fine table grapes all over the world.

High in the mountains of the Western Cape, the wind ripples through the fynbos (left). Many of the fynbos species have underground rootstocks which enable the plants to survive the veld fires that all too often devastate the mountains in the dry summer months. Despite their hardiness, however, the flowers display delicate floral structures that are a constant delight to botanists and the ever-growing numbers of hikers that are taking to the mountains.

Trellised vines cover the Hex River Valley (overleaf). There is a legend of a beautiful witch ('heks' in Dutch) who unwittingly sent her lover to his doom. Grief drove her insane and, on stormy nights, she is still said to wander abroad.

A female sugarbird (above) sips nectar from a pin-cushion protea (*Leucospermum cordifolium*). Proteas are probably the best known of all the great variety of South African flowers and form part of the typical south-western plant group known as fynbos (literally 'fine or delicate bush'), characterized by evergreen shrubs with hard, drought-resistant foliage. The leaves are usually very small, and the overall shade is a greenish-blue. The fynbos is one of the botanical wonders of the world, and despite the relatively small area it covers, is regarded as one of the six Floral Kingdoms. In the fynbos, more plant species occur per square kilometre than in any other part of the world.